Sight Fishing for Trout

To:

Harry,

Good luck on your sight
fishing adventures!

Tight Lines,

[signature]

Sight Fishing for Trout

Landon Mayer

STACKPOLE
BOOKS

To my mom, Roberta Lee Mayer-Skar, the woman who raised me to understand that love, morals, honesty, and respect would lead me to accomplish any goals that I set my mind to. With her devotion as a single mother and her dedication to raising my brother, Sean Mayer, my sister, Lauren Skar, and me, I was able to pursue my passion, career, and lifestyle. Following her example as a parent taught me to become the best father I can possibly be and a teacher to others.

Copyright © 2010 by Landon Mayer

Published by
STACKPOLE BOOKS
5067 Ritter Road
Mechanicsburg, PA 17055
www.stackpolebooks.com

Printed in China

10 9 8 7 6 5 4 3 2 1

First edition

Photography by the author unless otherwise noted

Library of Congress Cataloging-in-Publication Data

Mayer, Landon R.
    Sight fishing for trout / Landon R. Mayer. — 1st ed.
        p.   cm.
    Includes index.
    ISBN 978-0-8117-0551-6
    1. Trout fishing. I. Title.

SH687.M3425 2010
799.17'57—dc22

2009008960

Contents

Foreword

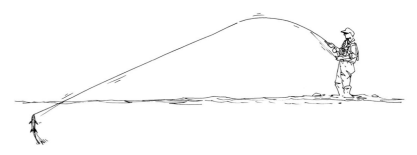

Most of us fish for trout without actually observing them—they're just a riseform on the surface, or they're somewhere below in the opaque water column, perhaps eating nymphs. We see the fish when it surfaces to take our fly or when our strike indicator dips with a take. But we should learn to "think with our eyes," the way the true predator does when it searches for food. That is the subject of Landon Mayer's new book.

When I taught my grandson to fly fish, I said to him, "Ben, you must learn to observe, to watch your fly as it floats, to think with your eyes. Otherwise you will not see the fish take your fly, and you will not be able to react fast enough to strike and hook the fish. Eventually you will habitually fix your eyes on the fly and react." I explained to him that we would go to a gin-clear stream where he could observe directly the feeding and other behaviors of trout, to learn about the fish he will try to catch. I explained to him that I had learned the most about trout by observing them in the clear waters of New Zealand. Then, I told him, I began to realize truths about trout that I had never understood before.

Trout are like chameleons: they naturally take on the colors of the stream bottom on which they dwell. They are drift feeders, facing upstream to take their food as it drifts to them. They are investigators, taking into their mouths every drifting tidbit and eating or rejecting it depending on its food value. They have no hands, so they must use their mouths to do the interception and taste testing.

They have feeding lies and hiding lies; one provides them with sustenance and the other with safety. Their sense of smell is much greater than ours, for the olfactory portions of their brains are more evolved than ours—occupying a larger percentage of their (tiny) brains. Wild trout are particularly alarmed by the smell of man; thus, in New Zealand guides always fish upcurrent of the trout.

Trout evolved as both predator and prey: As predator species they prey on drifting aquatic insects and fish. As prey species, they must be able to spot approaching predators from above (osprey and eagles) and below (mink and otter). Their eyesight is nearly full circle (and in all planes), so they can see in all directions except about 10 to 15 percent directly behind. As prey, external movement is their key alarm signal. Their entire bodies act as highly sensitive sound receivers, and wading sounds in quiet waters send them fleeing.

So where does this leave us as trout predators? As Robert Bachman learned in his three-year doctoral studies monitoring trout behavior, conducted on the Penn State University water on Spruce Creek, most wild trout disappeared from their feeding lies before expert fly fishers could approach the stream using stealth and camouflage clothing. Considering this, can we even hope to get close enough to wild adult stream trout to observe them—and catch them?

Yes, we can. There is an old fishing adage that says, "Ten percent of the fishermen catch 90 percent of the fish." The percentage is overstated. It is more accurate to assert that 10 percent of the fishermen catch 70 percent of the older trout, and they catch them by first locating them, observing their feeding behavior, and then selecting the right

John Randolph lifts a New Zealand brown that he caught by sight fishing. JOHN RANDOLPH

fly and presenting it the way the fish expects to see its prey. All of this successful predatory behavior is predicated on our experience. And the most important element of that experience is learning how to spot fish (especially trout in streams), and especially the largest, oldest specimens of the species.

Developing the eye of the hunter (coure d'oille) is key to successful trout spotting. If you are one of those hunters who can spot deer while speeding by woods, then you understand the concept of the "hunter's eye." Human physiologists explain the reaction of the human eye to tonal differences this way: if one differently colored M&M is placed on a traveling belt of uniformly colored M&M candies, the eye instantly picks out the fraud by tonal contrast. Once the hunter's eye learns to recognize prey shape (morphology), tone, shadow image and movements that "don't fit the surroundings," and preferred feeding and hiding locations, his search-image recognition and eye triggers are educated. He begins to think with his eyes. More than half his work is conditionally prescribed. The rest is stalking, spotting, and presentation.

Most successful hunters are born with inherent predatory instincts. They are *driven* to catch (or kill) a prey. Humans evolved as hunters, after all. But even nonhunters can become superb fishers through training, if they have enough drive to learn the elements of eye-search and recognition as explained by Landon Mayer. It helps to begin the eye training where large fish, especially trout

and steelhead (but also smallmouth bass), are found in clear water. Large steelhead enter Great Lakes tributary streams in spring and fall in preparation for spawning. The streams are often small, shallow, and clear, and the fish are many and large. These settings provide excellent opportunities to train your eyes to spot fish and to develop techniques for presenting flies to them, as well as hooking, playing, and releasing them.

What you learn by spotting and watching trout in clear water is that each trout has a distinct personality, much like humans and other animals. This makes fish watching more fascinating, a discipline in itself. Some trout prefer to feed left; others right. Some, in New Zealand for example (where there are no trout predators except humans), prefer to take naps, often in full daylight. Some seem to sulk or lie still. Others are extremely aggressive to fish intruders. Some feed languidly, others frenetically. Some are suckers for the dry; others feed almost exclusively on nymphs in their safe zone, that bottom six inches or foot of water where they feel safe. Others rise upward through the water column, feeding freely and comfortably at all levels.

Spring creeks are perhaps the best places to learn the disciplines of hunting with your eyes. The waters are clear and move slowly, and they produce large, older trout that have learned all the tricks of concealment and survival. Approaching these fish requires exceptional stealth. Perhaps it is the demanding hunting and fishing challenges of the spring creeks of the world that have produced our greatest trout fly anglers. Among those great spring-creek anglers, the one who taught me most in my decades of hunting and fishing for large trout was George Harvey of Pennsylvania, a born hunter and teacher. I think that George would have approved of this book by Landon Mayer, for it describes the psychology and the instinctive and learned skills of the true hunters of fish.

John Randolph
Editor-in-Chief, *Fly Fisherman*
September 3, 2008

Acknowledgements

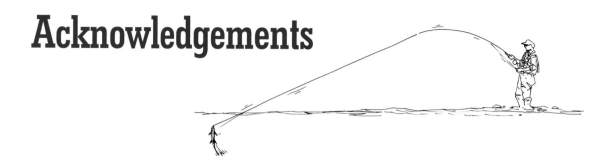

The one thing I have learned about the sport of fly fishing over the past eleven years as a full-time angler is that the adventure of the trip is what makes a day on the water a success. I also learned from other anglers—anglers I have come to know as remarkable individuals—that this sport is about giving before receiving—giving even the fish you just caught the chance to live and fight another day by returning it to the water.

This book would not be possible without the help of many great anglers and special individuals in the fly-fishing industry, many of whom have become good friends and lifelong fly-fishing partners.

I would like to thank my family and those close to me, including my daughter, Madelyn; Dominique Alvarado; and Jennifer O'Neal. Without the patience, understanding, and love from these three great ladies I would not have been able to complete this book. Thank you for making this possible.

Thank you to Judith Schnell for believing in me and in this project, and for providing others with the helpful tips and techniques that over the years have produced such great results. In addition, thanks to Debra Smith and all the others at Stackpole Books whose hard work is reflected in this book. It is truly an honor to work with such a professional team.

I would also like to thank Jay Nichols, without whose professionalism, honesty, friendship, and willingness to share this book would not be possible. Jay Nichols is one of the best editors, photographers, and anglers this sport has to offer. As he

has done for me, I will continue to do, passing on the same passion to achieve a goal while helping others along the way. Thank you for all your help and support.

John Barr is one of the kindest men I have ever known, on or off the water. John's experience in the sport of fly fishing is unsurpassed, and he has taught me to be a more patient angler in my pursuits on the river and throughout my career. His friendship and honesty has helped me shape my career; I will always treasure and follow in his path to help others.

Angus Drummond (Gus) is a good friend, great angler, and all-around stand-up individual. His eye for photography and sight fishing are reflected in the many great photographs in this book that capture moments we've shared on the water.

John Randolph, Ross Purnell, and Geoff Mueller from *Fly Fisherman* magazine, all great anglers and editors, made it possible for me to pursue my passion to help others and be successful every day on the water. I am thankful for everything they have done; I look forward to our future trips and projects together.

Peter Crowe, CEO and one of the masterminds of Smith Optics, shared his expertise in the field of polarized sunglasses that honestly made me a better sight fisherman. His knowledge and help are a great addition to this book.

Pat Dorsey, fellow guide, angler, and friend, and others on our home waters of the South Platte River, have brought many smiles to anglers over the years. Pat is a true professional in the sport of fly fishing, and I look forward to more adventures on the water with him.

Scottie Miller taught me a great deal about writing back when I worked on my first book, *How to Catch the Biggest Trout of Your Life*. An angler first, Scottie made the transition to author possible with his countless hours of dedication as a friend, editor, and giving individual. I will always be grateful to him, and I try to instill his teachings in every project I pursue. Thanks to him and his family for all the hard work.

My first published fly-fishing piece was made possible through *High Country Angler* magazine and Frank Martin. Whenever I need advice on anything from angling, parenting, or life, Frank has always been there. I thank him and his family for all their support.

Dave Hall, one of the industry's best illustrators, has helped many projects evolve to their highest potential, as he does here.

Special thanks to Eric Mondragon and Jay Harper. Thanks for the support over the years as friends and anglers, on or off the water. Your insight while I was writing this book helped the project move along at a productive pace.

To my friends and great anglers: without the days shared on the water, this book would not be possible. I thank you.

To the industry individuals, professionals, and companies who believed in my cause and in me: thank you. The support and gear make it possible to perform on the water every day. Thanks also to the fly shops and TU, FFF, and fly-fishing clubs who have supported me throughout my career.

Thanks to my sponsors: Cloudveil, Ross Reels/ Ross Worldwide, Rio Products, Smith Optics, Fishpond, Mad Trout Media, and Outcast Boats.

Finally, I would like to thank all the anglers who appreciated my work in this great industry. Your support makes it possible for me to follow this as a career. I hope this book brings you more success in your future fly-fishing adventures. I wish you all tight lines and many great sight-fishing experiences along the way.

Introduction

Fly fishing is my life. It is also how I make a living, and I cannot think of a better way to do so. A successful guide will not only get clients into fish, but will provide them with a challenging and rewarding experience so they return time after time. Over the years, I have found that there is no better way to do that than to show them the rewards of sight fishing for trout.

Sight fishing is a way to catch more and larger trout—trout that you can see in a river and that will be passed up by other anglers who cannot see them. Instead of relying on a strike indicator, you rely on a far more reliable indicator—the fish that you can see. You use your eyes to catch more fish; in turn, you are rewarded with seeing more of them strike your fly.

For years anglers have relied on reading the water to locate trout, and on drag-free or swinging drifts at different depths to trigger a take. This is blind fishing. It used to be reserved mostly for nymphing and streamer fishing, though prospecting with dry flies is also common. But those methods are not as effective as sight fishing—at least on the waters where I fish and guide. Over time, and due to water fluctuation, temperature changes, and pressure from anglers of all types, trout have become wise and have had to adjust to survive. Because of this pressure, trout are migrating and holding in new areas that were once thought of as nonproductive waters. In addition, these trout are more wary and less likely to move to take a fly. So accurate presentations are more critical.

One of the best ways to consistently catch larger fish is to focus on looking for them. JACK HANRAHAN

Sight fishing has been effective for decades in New Zealand, where it is common to walk a mile or more in between fish. A majority of the encounters in clear New Zealand waters are with large trout, making them easy to spot, but they are also some of the wariest trout to present a fly to. New Zealand anglers had to become accurate as individuals and teams in spotting the fish, approaching and getting into position while the fish remained happily holding in a run. Most important, the anglers had to make every presentation count. They typically got only one to three shots at the fish before they had to start walking again.

These New Zealand strategies and approaches to sight fishing are now useful and critical tools on many rivers in the United States, especially in tailwaters or small rivers, where it is difficult—or in most situations impossible—to have a good distance between you and the fish when you make a presentation. But you still have the upper hand. The guesswork of finding the fish is out of the equation, and you can get into the best possible position to catch the fish. Let's take a look at some of the advantages of sight fishing.

Catch more large fish. One of the best ways to consistently catch larger fish is to focus on looking for them. It's that simple. Many anglers go to a pool and hook fish after fish, all relatively small, and call it a day. They are happy because they have had plenty of action. If they catch a big one, all the better. The sight-fishing angler, though, makes his own luck and calls his own shots. You can't hunt big fish by shotgunning the water.

Take higher percentage shots. It is frustrating to see a fish in a run and know that you are making a good presentation—and the fish is simply not willing to take the fly. But not all fish are willing to eat. The advantage to seeing trout before you make a cast is that you are able to react to the fish's movements and behavior. If you know what a happy, feeding fish looks like, you will fish more efficiently, passing up the fish that are not interested.

Stay low and downstream of the trout so that you can get close to the fish without spooking it. A close-up look will let you know how the fish is behaving in the water so that you can determine if it is worth casting to.

Fish with confidence. If you can spot a fish, then you know you are not wasting your time blindly fishing the water. You know that every accurate presentation will be seen by the trout. This eliminates any second-guessing you may have for each drift. The key is to make sure the fish can see your presentation by drifting it through the feeding lane and not letting the current take your fly from the fish's view. By reading the fish's behavior, you can confidently adjust your techniques.

Spook fewer fish. One reason that a small percentage of anglers catch most of the fish is because most anglers spook the fish before they ever have the opportunity to cast. If you know that the fish is directly in front of you, or right at the river's edge, you approach the water with more caution and you will see more trout. Those are the trout that would spook if you rushed up to a run and starting blind-casting through it.

Fish areas that other anglers pass up. This is my favorite part of sight fishing. You arrive at a famous western tailwater. Several cars are in the parking lot, and the river is dotted with anglers at every bend. For many anglers this is a deterrent, and they leave to find other water to fish. But when you are good at sight fishing, you learn to check the water between the conventional fishing spots. The pools may be crowded, but you can have the rest of the river to yourself all day.

Learn about presentation. You want every presentation to count. If you can see the fish and see your flies, you know immediately if your cast is off target, and you can adjust. By watching the drift of the fly, you learn how the currents affect your presentation, and you can make appropriate changes. By gauging the fish's reactions and watching how your fly moves through the water, you teach yourself how to present the fly under a wide

Fishing blind is not wrong, bad, or ineffective. When you come across a great piece of water that has all of the right elements but you can't see any fish, it is certainly worth a few drifts through the run. But there is a lot more to fishing than that.

variety of conditions. Watching the fly and the fish, for instance, taught me that while traditional techniques may work, unconventional techniques also work. Drag-free drifts in many situations are productive, but not always. I learned that normal casting motions spook fish and that indicators do not really relay strikes. The fly is not the most important subject in the equation—the trout is.

Catch more fish. At the end of the day, you will catch more fish because you fish smarter. You cover more water in the course of one day, giving you more opportunities to catch trout instead of targeting only the fish holding in a few runs.

While I'm guiding, I love watching an angler transition from using only conventional methods of blind fishing to adding sight fishing to their store of techniques. The thrill and excitement of using this approach can leave you sleepless at night and ready for more, especially when you are hunting trophy-sized trout.

In the winter of 2007 a client and friend of mine, John Nash, booked three courageous days on the water, battling low flows and winter weather. Despite that, John and I decided to give the trip a green light. The first day was a success, getting some of the rust off that had accumulated during the cold winter. With a few quality fish in the net, John and I were clicking as a team. I knew the days to come would get even better, and we'd see more trout in the low water conditions.

While the flows were still low on the second day, the water began to clear and the sun came out, making it easier to see the fish. John's excitement over seeing the trout actually take his fly was priceless. He was pumped—and we knew the next day was the last chance to see the trophy he was searching for.

We did get a break on day three—not much, but the flows jumped up thirty cubic feet per second. The weather was a mix of sun and snow with some wind. From a teaching point of view, this was great; I could show John tips for different weather conditions. I was feeling good.

With time and practice, sight fishing pays off. John Nash is rewarded for his passion and time on the water.

That morning, the sky was dark with moisture clouds, and the water's surface reflected the dark conditions, giving us superb visibility, which we would not have had in sunny or white-cloud conditions. We started way downriver. I was ahead of John, scanning every bit of the deep runs. Just as I was ready to pass through a run, something caught my eye. It looked like a slight movement of a dorsal fin.

I motioned to John to stop and I quickly dropped to my knees. He looked at me in disbelief. I quietly said, "Yes," with an arm gesture, "I found them," as I crawled back to the area where John had stopped dead in his tracks. Three huge 'bows were stacked side by side at the very bottom of a deep, 7-foot run. Prespawn fish are the biggest and most challenging trout to see in any river because they haven't yet colored up.

With John at my left, I pointed to the small pod of giants and told him we would drift above the trout to see if they were eager to take our flies. We both breathed deeply, and then I prepared John to get ready for a downstream battle if he hooked one. These beasts were big.

After a few practice casts downstream, and a few drifts without a hookup, there it was—a slight hesitation, followed by a smooth lift of the rod. The trout when nuts: arm-thrusting head shakes, a nice cartwheel out of the water, and a 100-plus-yard bolt downstream. Finally John was face-to-face with what he was waiting for. Breathing heavily, red in the face, and with the biggest grin ever, he turned and said, "You told me he would be pissed, but that was an understatement!" We ended the day with a 9-pound chrome female, a 10-pound buck, and topped it off with a cherry: a 12-pound bruiser. It was a historic trip for both of us.

The gratification you feel from spotting the trout, watching it take your fly, and seeing it erupt to the surface doesn't pass quickly. Watching a trout heavier than 10 pounds slowly open its mouth to suck in a midge will give an adrenaline rush to even the dry-fly purists.

Although trout have brains the size of a pea, they can make any angler feel humble. You can never know enough; every day there is something the river and the trout can teach you. So the next time you're out on the water, take in all you see, and let the trout tell you what to do.

When sight fishing, let the trout tell you what to do. By gauging the fish's reactions and watching how your fly moves through the water, you teach yourself how to present the fly under a wide variety of conditions.

Low light allows trout to feel secure and feed without pressure, but the low-angled sun also makes it hard to spot trout. This is when any advantage you can give yourself will help you catch more trout.

CHAPTER 1

Windows of Opportunity

Spotting trout is one of the hardest fly-fishing skills to learn. Just like one of those three-dimensional pictures you have to stare at for a while before the image appears, trout blend in with their surroundings so well that you have to learn how to look at the water in a special way before they become visible. Sometimes trout seem like they are part chameleon. Add to that disguise the moving currents, varying lighting conditions, and the sometimes impossible glare on the water, and you can understand why spotting fish in the water can be difficult. But it is worth practicing because if you can spot fish when the lighting is bad, you have an enormous advantage over other anglers.

Glare is a fairly broad term that is used to describe several different things, all of which affect your ability to see. There are two types of glare on the water: direct and reflected. Direct glare is the blindness that you experience when you are looking out on the water while facing in the direction of the sun. Reflected glare is the sometimes impenetrable coat of light over the surface of water that prevents you from looking into it. All sorts of things, including the sun and clouds (two of the biggest culprits), are reflected off the mirrorlike surface of the water. Though glare is part of being on the river, there are ways to get around it, or rather *see through* it. Glare is your worst enemy when you are scanning water: early or late in the day when there is tough glare on the water; on white cloud-filled days that reflect white on the surface; and in early spring or late fall when glistening, white, snow-filled banks reflect on the water. All of these blinding conditions make it impossible to see trout in the water.

A good pair of polarized glasses will help you combat glare. JACK HANRAHAN

The first thing that you need is a good pair of polarized glasses, which I discuss in chapter 6. Dark objects are less apt to reflect light because the pigments of the color absorb light rather than reflecting it back to your eyes. Finding ways to control light reflecting up into your face gives you a huge advantage. The following are things you can do or wear to help stop the glare from below when you are hunting trout.

- Make sure the bottom of the brim of your hat is a dark color.
- Pick frames and models of glasses that cover the sides of your eyes thoroughly.
- Wear a hood or beanie large enough so that you can pull it down over a baseball cap, making it seem like you are looking out of a dark room.
- Place your arm underneath your chin to block unwanted rays, or use a balaclava, Buff, or dark neck warmer.
- Keep the sun at your back.

We will review these in more detail later in the book. In this chapter I explain what anglers call viewing lanes, and how to take advantage of them when you find them. Along the same lines as viewing lanes are viewing windows, which are prime spots that allow you to look into the water. I cover these in more detail in chapter 5, when I discuss some prime spots to look for trout.

Viewing lanes are large, glare-free areas that provide good views of the river bottom. These lanes can come from sun (both the presence or absence of it, and the angle at which the light hits the water), shadows, structure, and sky coloration. Within these viewing lanes are windows—spots that provide good opportunities for you to look into the water. One of the secrets to spotting fish is to learn how to use viewing lanes and windows. Finding these viewing lanes is part of a larger process of learning how to look at the trout stream in a different way in order to see, and eventually catch, more fish.

A viewing lane is nothing more than a section of water without glare. It can be upstream, downstream, or directly in front of you, and it can span anywhere from a few feet to all the way across the river. Viewing lanes are formed in a variety of

When there are a large number of trout holding in calm water with a clear viewing lane all the way across the river, always try to prevent any additional movement to the line, your body, or anything that might cause even the slightest disturbance and spook the trout.

ways, but the most common is when the source of the glare (the sun and other distracting reflections) is eliminated from the water. When you find one, you can use it to spot fish; it will give you the upper hand.

High Sun

A high sun (an hour before and after noon) combined with blue skies provide the best possible viewing lanes. Light is not at an angle and bouncing into your eyes, offering you a view of the entire stream bottom. As long as you keep the sun at your back, you will see fish that would be invisible to you in low light or cloudy conditions. You will never get a larger viewing lane than on bluebird

High, stained water often draws in new fresh fish that are difficult to see, but the rewards of sight fishing in these conditions are worth it. This char/Dolly Varden was caught by Eric Mondragon after searching for a fish in dirty water.

This is a great example of a viewing lane from a strip of dark sky reflecting on the water's surface. The lane stretches all the way across the river.

John Barr holds a brown that took a Tungstone in bright sun. High sun provides the largest viewing windows, though the fish are often spooky.

sunny days. If the trout are difficult to see when the sun is at a low angle, wait until high noon to sight-fish. Then you will have at least an idea of where to look for fish in poor light conditions.

As a bonus, fish activity increases on sunny days during colder weather; as the sun rises, the water temperatures increase and the trout are more active. This activity, even if it is only the fin movement of a trout lying on the bottom of a run, is enough to reveal the fish. But sunlight makes it easy to spook it. The easier it is for you to see the trout, the easier it is for the trout to detect any movement from above.

Friendly Skies

One paradox in the sight-fishing game is that sunny days are best for spotting trout, but they also make trout more wary, almost impossible to catch.

Cloudy days, on the other hand, are great for fishing but can make it extremely difficult to spot fish. As a working guide, I am on the water in all sorts of conditions and need to roll with what Mother Nature delivers.

The two worst sky conditions where I fish in Colorado are an abundance of puffy white clouds or a sheet of gray clouds. Those powder days that skiers love make sight fishing an enormous challenge. Low, gray skies act in the same way as the hazy skies typical of East Coast summers. But weather changes quickly, especially out West, and even a slight change can give you a break. Some days when light-gray clouds fill the sky and you can't see because of the glare—all of a sudden blue sky breaks through the clouds, providing a short-lived window to see into the water. On other days, glare from a late-afternoon sun makes sight fishing difficult, but then a dark cloud rolls in and reflects the dark sky onto the water's surface, giving you a clear window into the water.

The ideal situation for a viewing lane is dark skies, whether it is the whole sky above or just a part of the sky. This dark reflection eliminates all the glare on the river's surface and the river bottom will be easy to see—as clear in the dark, reflected areas of the river as it is at high noon on sunny days. Such times are a double bonus because not only can you see better but the fish are also happy to have the cloud cover.

Cloud-filled skies makes for some of the most challenging sight fishing. There is so much glare from the white clouds reflecting off the surface that your viewing lane might be only three feet in front of you. Since your vision is limited, you can't distinguish fish silhouettes (the first thing that I look for) or color (unless it is a really bright-colored fish), and you have to look for movement. On the other hand, trout are more active and less wary, so their movements are easier to spot, and they certainly respond better to flies.

Cloudy conditions with lots of glare makes it so hard to see that you spook a lot more fish—you simply can't see far enough ahead of you. But just because you spook a fish doesn't mean that you can't catch it. After the fish spooks, try to follow where it went—if it is a large fish, you might see its wake. When the fish stops, approach it cautiously. If you lose sight of the fish, wait a few minutes; most of the time the trout will return to its feeding lane.

As a general rule, large, migratory fish that have entered the river from a lake, reservoir, or ocean will settle down faster than wild year-round stream residents. The key is to not rush a cast to the moving target. Wait until the fish settles down, and then try a presentation. If you can't see the fish, for instance if it is in the late evening or early morning, make a cast short of the last area where you saw the wake. Many anglers do not realize that most of the trout hooked in these conditions have spooked before any casts are made. In some cases,

if the fish hadn't spooked, you would not even know it was there.

Shadows

One thing is for sure: trout are not afraid of the dark. Large browns hunker down during the day and become predators at night. All trout love shadows where they find refuge while they feed. These areas supply great cover from predators.

During the late afternoon, the sun drops and shadows lengthen, creating great lanes to see the

White clouds provide the worst conditions for spotting trout because the water reflects the white. Slow down and thoroughly scan the water in these conditions.

Dark skies during the first or last hour of daylight make the reflection on the water's surface almost disappear. This is when you will find more trout, and they are not wary of any predators from above.

fish. For example, tall lodgepole pines along the riverbank cast long shadows, stretching almost all the way across the river. On the other hand, a small patch of willows lining the run make a shadow that fish will feed in. I have seen giant trout find comfort in only a foot-long shadow.

However, a disadvantage to these magic hours is that your own shadows are more prominent. To prevent spooking a wary trout, adjust your positioning on the water and approach the area with a low profile—and I mean low. I have had to cast while lying down.

When you find a shadowed area to target fish, you have to be in that shadowed area as well. You will not see very well if you are in a bright area, trying to look into a dark one. When you are fishing in a canyon, finding shadows is relatively easy because of the high walls. When I am fishing the Dream Stream, which is more or less open, shadows are harder to find. In some instances, I look for a shadow from a 5-foot-high willow on the

river's edge. In this situation, I go to the side of the river where the fish is holding and get downstream of the fish in the same shadow. Once I spot the fish, I find a marker directly in line with where the fish is holding—such as a rock or a branch or whatever—and then move across stream, into the light, to make the presentation. This is the best way that I know of to catch brown trout in the fall, when trout are only willing to come out of hiding to feed in the shadows. When the river is shadowless, the fish remain in cover.

Polarized glasses with brown or copper tints are really helpful in these situations. One theme that I will revisit time and time again is this: when you are looking for trout in extremely difficult situations, most of the time you are only going to see a part of the fish. So when I am looking into shadows, which is difficult because of the dark environment, the high contrast of the copper, brown, or amber tints works better than extremely light yellow tints or dark gray tints. Look for a part of

On extremely bright days in clear water on freestone rivers, shadows provide the best viewing lanes.

a fish, such as colors (the reds, greens, and blues), or body parts, such as the top of a dorsal fin or the tip of a tail. If you can see one part of the fish, you can judge where its head is and make your presentation.

Bridges often provide the only shade on the river when the sun is high, and they attract fish at these times. Trout find refuge in shadows cast on the water by trees or cliffs. Another type of shadow is one that is cast by your body. Here is a common situation: Around 3 or 4 o'clock in the afternoon you are walking upstream and having difficulty finding fish because of the angled sun on the

Objects reflected onto the water can create viewing lanes. The impenetrable glare can change to a color that you can see through.

In cloudy conditions with lots of glare on the water, it is important to find a viewing lane, whether large or small, and then scan the water thoroughly.

water. Your viewing lanes have decreased to two feet in front of you because of the glare from the low-angled sun. At the same time, the low-angled sun creates long shadows off your body. These shadows walk ahead of you and spook fish ... but not always. If you walk slowly enough, instead of spooking the fish, your shadow may make the fish easier to see. You must move extremely slowly to prevent spooking fish. It is risky, but it is better than nothing and works for me often enough to pass the tip along to you. It is more effective for fish in deep water that are less spooky than fish in shallow water.

This is a prime example of how structure, in this case overhanging trees, creates a viewing lane on the river. This particular viewing lane stretches halfway across the river.

Eric Mondragon searches a viewing lane in Alaska to find egg-eating rainbow trout among the sockeye salmon. Even with a stain in the water, this viewing lane is wide enough to let him see halfway across the river.

Large, colorful maple trees throw their shadow along this slate-bottom steelhead stream in Pennsylvania. John Barr spotted a chromer taking advantage of this hiding spot. JAY NICHOLS

Structure

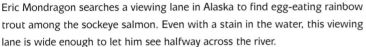

Structure is always a good place to look for trout, because the trout rely on those areas for safety and cover. However, structure has an added benefit when sight-fishing. The color of the objects—whether it is a patch of willows or trees lining the river's edge—act like a dark cloud, allowing good visibility into the river. The best times for this are in summer when the leaves are deep green and throw a dark reflection on the river. This is incredibly helpful in bright and cloudy conditions or wide-open landscapes when spotting trout is challenging. It is always easier to see into dark areas of the river than sections that reflect bright glare off the water's surface.

Dark structure such as the high slate walls on Pennsylvania steelhead streams or dark green conifers reflecting onto the water creates excellent viewing lanes. Conversely, reflections on the water from some foliage, such as blazing red and orange maples and yellow aspens in the fall, can wreak havoc on your vision. Reflections from snowbanks also ruin visibility.

Another way to increase your viewing lane is to look from a high vantage point, such as a bank, bridge, or even by climbing a tree. But, and this is absolutely critical, high vantage points are just that—places to look from, but not places to fish from. After looking from a high bank or a bridge, get down and get into the water or into a low position before you start casting. Anglers often try to cast from the high spot because it is so tempting (how many times have you entertained yourself by trying to cast to trout from a bridge?), but you should mark the fish and move into a better position. These high vantage points are critical when you are using the buddy system, covered in chapter 15.

Once you have the tools to reduce glare, you have to train your eyes to spot fish. JAY NICHOLS

In the Zone

Finding a good viewing lane is half the battle. Next comes training your eyes to look for fish. We constantly focus our eyes during the day: when reading a paper, staring at the computer screen, and so on. While focusing in such a way is necessary, sometimes the ability to use our peripheral vision becomes dull. Concentrating on one thing for a long time not only takes a lot of energy, but it is a distraction when you try to function in a dynamic environment. When someone encourages you to focus on the task at hand or focus on a goal, they might say, "Don't take your eyes off the ball." But in reality, the best ball players see a wide range of things throughout the game, honing in when they hit the ball or shoot the shot. This seemingly psychic ability to know what is going on all around them is a phenomenon that some call "field sense."

Granted, this is fly fishing, not professional baseball. But the ability to suspend your normal way of looking and rely on other ways of seeing instead can greatly improve your success rate. This means learning to shift your focus, being more aware of what is going on in your peripheral vision, and relying on your hearing. All of these give you a heightened sense of awareness, which is what I think must, at least partially, be what athletes often refer to as being "in the zone."

Shifting Focus

One of the biggest problems that I have when taking photographs around water is that when I point my camera at a fish in the water, the camera focuses on the surface of the water (or something else), and the fish is out of focus. To take control of the shot, I have to manually focus the camera—turn off autofocus if it's the program mode—and tell the camera to focus on the fish. In

I caught this fish using a rig set up with a strike indicator, but I only used the indicator to suspend the fly in the water while I focused my attention on the fish to determine when to set the hook.

program mode, the camera, though a sophisticated piece of equipment, cannot figure out that my true subject is beneath the surface of the water.

The camera's computer is similar to our own brain when we are confronted with a situation like this. Many of us arrive on the stream in program mode, if you will, and we focus on the surface of the water rather than on what we really need to be focusing on—the trout.

The most common vision inhibitor is the strike indicator. What most anglers do is this: they get to the water, approach a run, and start fishing. They immediately focus on that strike indicator. This narrowing of focus—this tunnel vision—occurs way too early in the game and inhibits the angler's ability to see what is going on around him. Not only does it dull your senses, but you rob yourself of many of the thrills of the sight-fishing game.

That is not to say that indicators are evil. Good anglers who know how to fish with strike indicators look past the indicator to see the fish and its reactions in the water. A fish's reactions are a far better and more reliable indicator of a take than the float. This ability to look past the surface of the water, and to look past the indicator while still keeping it in view, is an important skill to develop. It is what I call shifting your focus.

Try this simple experiment: Go to a room in your house with a favorite picture on the wall, and stand 10 feet back from it. Extend your arm out from you and point your finger up like a number one sign so that it is directly between you and the picture. Now stare at your finger, concentrating on counting the creases around your knuckle. Then focus on the painting, appreciating all of the things that you like about it, while keeping your finger in view. This ability to look past something, while still retaining it in view, is what I mean by shifting your focus.

It's the same as looking at one of those 3-D images—the ones that look like a bunch of noise but after looking at them in a special way, a three dimensional image appears. The secret to seeing the picture is to look past the picture. The trick is to not focus on the plane of the paper, but to force your eyes to unfocus and look beyond it. People have shared many tips on how to learn how to see these pictures, and one of the most interesting that I have heard is the dirty window technique: look outside through a dirty window, then focus on the dirt on the window, then on the outside, and keep alternating your focus between what is outside and the spot on the glass. You can feel and memorize how your focus moves. This is the shift in focus that I am talking about.

To do something similar on-stream, find a highly visible rock on the bottom of the run. Concentrate on the rock for more than a minute (similar to how long you would look at a trout before you make a presentation). Then refocus on the whole section of water so that you can see the river bottom while keeping the rock in view. This is exactly how you approach a trout: focus first on the fish, then refocus on the run to make an accurate cast, then focus back on the trout to see the take.

What does this have to do with catching more fish? When we read words on a page or look at a computer screen all day, as many of my clients do, we train our eyes to focus on one thing and stop there. This exercise helps you look beyond where your eyes want to instinctively focus. If you can train yourself to look past the surface distractions and see more of the trout stream, you will see more fish. If you can see more fish, you have the potential to catch more of them.

Just one trout is not enough to make you stop shifting your gaze. You might need to look past that fish as well. You need to stay calm and not cast at the first fish you see. Experienced big fish hunters,

This fat rainbow is a great reward. Looking past the bright glare of sun on the water's surface, I was able to see the trout and make a correct presentation. ANGUS DRUMMOND

whether for trout or tarpon, have the uncanny ability to quickly survey a pool or pod of fish and discern the big one.

In addition to shifting focus, there is something else: it is more like an ability to defocus the eyes, or not really look at anything specific while you search the water. Just like a hunter scanning the woods or a bird-watcher scanning the brush for a bird only 4 inches long, you don't focus on every little thing. Instead you scan the water looking for movement or inconsistencies in the surroundings that might indicate a fish. This leads us to another aspect of our vision: peripheral vision.

Peripheral Awareness

Peripheral vision is what you are able to see outside of the very center of your gaze, which is called foveal vision. The numbers vary, but according to studies by NASA, an individual's peripheral vision extends about 167 degrees with the head and eyes fixed. If the subject rotates his head and eyes, that

Even when fishing to a particular target, you should still be aware of what is going on in your peripheral vision.
JACK HANRAHAN

vision extends to an amazing 237 degrees, allowing him to literally see behind himself. You can quickly gauge your own peripheral vision by looking straight ahead at a fixed point on a wall at eye level. Extend your arms straight out from your sides, and point your fingers. If your arms are extended straight out at your sides, that is 180 degrees. Can you see your fingers? If not, bring them in a little toward the front.

Peripheral vision, also called side vision, is good at picking up movement, but poor at picking up colors. This is a function of how the eye is built. The retina has two types of photoreceptors, rods and cones. Cones, which are densely packed in the center of the eyes, pick up color; rods, which are denser outside of the central part of the retina, are responsible for night vision, motion detection, and peripheral vision.

We use our peripheral vision every day—when merging onto a highway, or just catching a glimpse of an attractive person out of the corner of the eye. Since the number of rods and cones is fixed, we probably cannot improve our peripheral vision, but we can learn to use it more efficiently.

Studies have shown that handball players, for instance, have more or less the same peripheral vision as non-athletes. However, in the same studies, their reaction times were much quicker than the non-athletes. Peripheral awareness can be developed, and athletes and other people who rely on their full range of vision have a higher degree of awareness of what is going on in their peripheral vision. People who stare at a computer screen all day, which, unless it is a super widescreen, falls mostly in the center of their sight, are not really processing much from their periphery. Add some cubicles to the equation, and you pretty much eliminate the need to process information from the side.

What does this have to do with fishing? Several things. Instead of just looking for clues in the water right in front of you, develop your peripheral vision and you can extend your viewing range sig-

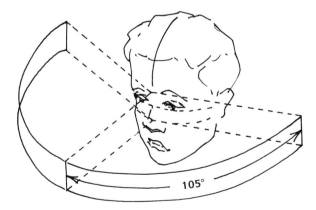

Range of peripheral vision.

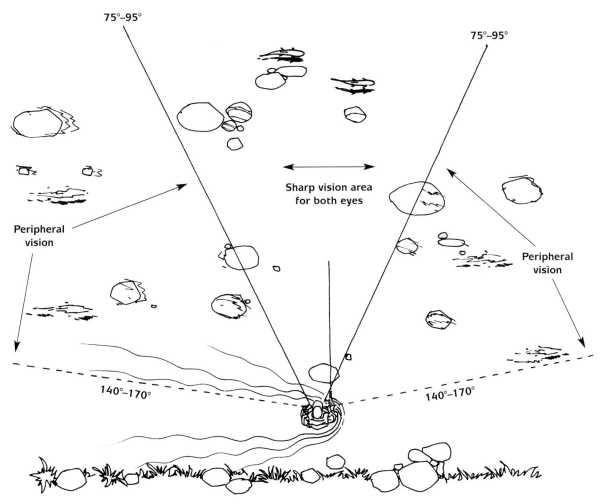

75°–95°

75°–95°

Sharp vision area
for both eyes

Peripheral
vision

Peripheral
vision

140°–170°

140°–170°

Peripheral vision on the water.

nificantly. You may not be able to focus on something that you see out of your peripheral vision, but if you have a wider field of vision, you will see, and therefore filter, a wider range of clues. Additionally, motion, which is one area in which peripheral vision excels, is one of the best ways to spot fish. Trout are always moving some part of their body—whether aggressively to take food, or subtly to hold their position in the current.

Just as when you are driving down the road taking in a wide range of visual clues in front of you, such as exit signs or brake lights, and to your side, such as other cars in the next lane, you need to capitalize on your entire field of vision. Tunnel vision is the medical term for the loss of peripheral vision, and it is often used as a metaphor to describe someone who is so focused on one thing that he ignores everything else. Not a good thing when you are searching for trout. Only when you have selected your target should you focus on it and not pay attention to other things, which at that point have become a distraction.

After I find a viewing lane and then find a fish, I don't stop using my peripheral vision. I continue to look through the water to focus on the river bottom, keeping both the fish and the fly in my peripheral vision. Only after the cast do I switch my focus to the fish.

To cover lots of water efficiently, keep your eyes open as long as possible and concentrate on the area in your peripheral view while maintaining your normal walking speed. If you walk at a normal pace while scanning the river, you immediately increase your chances of locating trout because you are covering so much water. It's simple math. The more fish you spot, the more fish you can cast to—therefore, the more fish you catch.

Catching fish has as much to do with not spooking them as it does with making a successful presentation. I am an accomplished sight fisher, and I still spook a lot of fish. But I spot more than I spook. That lets me slow down, get low, and move into position to get a shot at them. These are all

fish that would have darted for cover if I just ambled along the bank, moving from pool to pool. If you can't spot them ahead of time, you spook them without even knowing they were there.

One of the best ways to practice identifying movement with your peripheral vision is to find a distant object in the river and practice using your side vision. While keeping your eyes centered on the object, try to see other objects downstream and upstream out of the corners of your eyes. Do this every time you go fishing, and every time, try to increase your range of view. Over time, you will see other parts of the river in your entire field of view, and you will be more efficient at hunting trout.

As a side note, it is uncomfortable to search water all day with your eyes wide open. Sunglasses help reduce strain from bright sun, but when you are using your peripheral vision, you blink less because you are trying to view a large surrounding

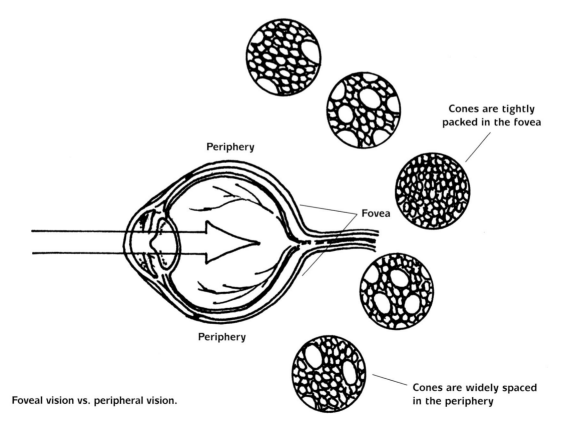

Periphery

Periphery

Fovea

Cones are tightly packed in the fovea

Cones are widely spaced in the periphery

Foveal vision vs. peripheral vision.

As you stalk a fish, the more you are aware of your surroundings, the less likely you are to spook other fish in the stream. JACK HANRAHAN

area. Your eyes dry out and feel irritated; sometimes it feels like your eyes are going to pop out of your head by the end of the day. A large bottle of Visine is part of my normal equipment, and it is a huge relief for dry eyes.

One Eye Closed

Rumor has it that pirates wore eye patches so that one eye would always be adapted to the dark in case they needed to work below decks or go into a night battle. If they were working on deck in the bright sun and had to go below to the dark holds, they would look with the eye which was covered with the eye patch. Some astronomers recommend wearing an eye patch over their observing eye while they are setting up their equipment, so that eye is completely dark-adapted when it is time to look through the telescope. Let's take a look at why this works, and then look at what in the world it has to do with fly fishing.

As I mentioned before, the retina has two types of cells: rods and cones. Cones, which are concentrated in the center, detect detail and color and work best in light. Rods are more or less for black and white, and low resolution; they detect movement and faint lights; and they come into play in peripheral and night vision. After your eyes have been exposed to something bright, it takes them a long time (20 minutes or more) to adjust back to being able to see in the dark. Interestingly, the shift from dark to light doesn't take as much time.

In Colorado where I fish, it is usually sunny and extremely bright. In the winter, the snowy banks are blinding. Yet we are always looking into water that, compared to the surroundings, is very dark. This is a problem. If your eyes are trained on the dark water, they adjust accordingly. If you have to move upstream and you look away from the dark stream and at the ground or sky as you walk, your eyes start to adjust to the light. This happens relatively quickly, but when your eyes

Bright sun reflecting off snowy banks can create blinding lighting conditions. ANGUS DRUMMOND

look back at the dark water, they take a considerable amount of time to readjust. Not only are you wasting precious fish-spotting time, but you spook more fish because you can't see them while your eyes are adjusting.

The solution is not an eye patch (the pirate look has not quite caught on in fly fishing). Shut one eye when you are on the move and then open it once you are back on the river. Since that eye does not have to adjust, you will see fish again right away. This technique is a huge help when I am traveling upstream in pursuit of fish, especially since a good number of trout like to hold on the river's edge where they can easily obtain food under cover.

Stop, Wait, and Listen

Hearing is a powerful sense, but it is under-used when hunting top-water feeders. One of the best sounds on the river during a thick hatch is the deep-pitched sipping sound of a large trout. When a fish tips its snout just above the water's surface,

you hear from a fair distance the suction when it opens its gills and sips in the fly.

This also happens when the trout aggressively crashes a caddis or hopper fluttering on the surface. I remember the time two friends and I hiked into the Black Canyon of the Gunnison to cast giant stoneflies to large, wild trout in mid-June, when the stonefly activity can be phenomenal. We hiked in the two-mile trail to our camping destination, set down our gear, and began rigging for the few hours of daylight we had left before we set up camp. I began to hear, every now and then, intense splashes on the water, and I immediately stopped rigging and looked for a jumbo-sized ring, those tell-tale ripples on the water. Needless to say, rigging took longer than usual. We decided to wade on the theory that the trout felt a lot of pressure from boats floating downstream in the middle of the river, which would push the trout to the river's edge where we would be in casting range. In the end, our theory was right—with a little twist.

After the first afternoon, we set up camp and talked about our strategy for the following day over some beer and good campfire grub. We decided to hike a ways upstream to a section of the river where there are steep rock cliffs that slide into the river. We had to swim around some of the structure, which added more adventure to our trip. All the while, we could occasionally hear heavy crashes somewhere on the water.

After thorough scanning, we discovered it was the sound of big trout crashing on the stoneflies falling in the shadows of the rock ledges. Even more impressive were the trout that would leap out of the water in an attempt to eat a hearty meal off the rock. This was one of the coolest things I have seen a trout do to get a meal. Clued in by our ears, verified with our eyes, we hit the walls with our flies for the remainder of the trip.

Sounds play a large role in sight fishing. I cannot even count the number of times I have stopped while leisurely walking upstream after hearing one of these sounds. When casting dry

High water and the abundance of shade for the fish to hide in made it essential to rely on sound as clues to the fishes' location.

flies to a trout and hearing a gulp, I'll stop dead in my tracks to scan the water's surface until I find the culprit.

Making the Transition

While some anglers have the advantage of being on the river on a regular basis, others stare at other objects more than they look into the water. If you are hitting the water after a week-long tour in the office (some of my clients fish only a handful of times each year), here are some tips for making the transition to the water and getting in the zone.

Slow down

One reason we go fishing is to escape stress, and indeed you generally won't fish well until you slow down and relax. This might take an hour—or even a few days if you are on a longer trip—before you start to slow down and get into the groove. When you are onstream, the first thing you should do is walk slowly. Catching a few fish and gaining confidence also helps. You might want to practice the controlling line, casting, presentations, and eye exercises before you start sight fishing.

Practice seeing

Spotting trout is not easy; it takes dedication and practice to see better every time on the water. Water movement, trout's ability to blend in with their surroundings, and varying light conditions make every day a new challenge. Because of this, I have learned to *practice* looking for trout every time I am on the river to teach myself how to find them in different conditions and settings.

Start below or at the end of the shallow run that you are beginning to scan and let your eyes adjust to the new water. I do this by picking a rock, vegetation, or simply an object in the river and I pretend that it is a trout. I scan the water up to the structure and then focus on it. Do this on a regular basis throughout the day: you are training your eyes to adjust.

Peripheral vision is connected with a relaxed state of mind, and some therapists use peripheral vision exercises to help their clients reduce stress.

When you first get to the water, make it a priority to spot a fish. You will have more confidence and know what to look for in the stream.

The beauty of this photograph is not just capturing the great trout in the image. It is also capturing the satisfaction of the angler enjoying the experience of his trip.

They have the client pick a spot on a wall slightly above eye level and then slowly extend their field of vision until they can see out of the corner of their eyes. Then they coach their clients through a visualization process, asking them to try to extend their field of awareness to 360 degrees. Even though you can't literally see behind you, some argue that this process, when conducted for several minutes, will slow your breathing, relax the muscles in your face, and perhaps even relax your entire body.

Be observant

Because one of the best ways to spot fish is to get a glimpse of something out of the ordinary, start to build a database in your mind of what ordinary is. It is easier to find fish in your home water because you are familiar with it. Early in a trip, gather as much data as possible, paying attention to what

fish look like when you do spot them. Don't just operate on autopilot. Even if you spook a few fish, you learn a lot about what to be looking for in the future. Trout never look the same in every river—some host bright colors, some are light or chrome with no color, some are dark to match their surroundings, while others seem to melt into the river bottom. Having a picture in your head will build the confidence you need. Having the confidence of knowing what to look for is critical.

The first thing to do when you get to the river is to locate a trout, and then keep that image stuck in the back of your mind as a reminder of what you will be looking for as the day wears on. Locate a clear, deep section of water that has trout in it and study the fish in that easily viewed area. The location doesn't have to be ideal for fishing. Instead, look for a spot that will give you this confidence-building visual. If it is not easy to see the fish because of water clarity or the lack of a high vantage point, walk to the edge of a run and stare into it while moving along the river's edge in order to deliberately spook a trout—you at least will be able to get that confidence-building image to help you see more fish.

One of the best ways to learn how to spot more fish is to have the discipline to walk the river without a fly rod and reel for the sole purpose of seeing as many trout as you can. Watching fish this way, without the urgency to make a presentation, allows you to observe the trout and its behavior in its natural environment.

Practice by going to locations where it is easy to see fish. Bridges are the easiest places, but high riverbanks provide a good view of fish and their behavior. Good examples are some of the waters located in my home state of Colorado, such as the Taylor River, Frying Pan River, Blue River, and the four main tailwater drainages of the South Platte: Elevenmile Canyon, Spinney Mountain Ranch, Cheesman Canyon, and Decker's.

In tailwaters such as the South Platte, every section of the river tailing out below the different reservoirs is a unique setting, each different from the last. For example, Cheesman Canyon has high red-rock canyon walls with large boulders throughout the course of the river, and Spinney Mountain Ranch is a winding river in a giant valley with big sky surrounded by the Rocky Mountains. Looking for fish in different river settings, different colors of river bottoms, and different lighting situations will help you recognize the different images of trout you will see on different sections of water. Once you have seen trout under these different conditions, you will forever have more confidence because you have the images in the back of your mind.

Lastly, try to locate trout during different times of the day. The difference between how a trout behaves and feeds in a run at high noon compared with its behavior during the last few hours of the day, when it has more cover and is not pressured

Brown trout are very good at hiding. Knowing this, be sure to make the right presentation to each fish and you may hook an aggressive brown trout like this male.

or nervous, is amazing. Over time, these techniques will help you become a better sight angler.

Think differently

It may seem corny, but try to put yourself in the fish's position—think about what it needs to survive and how it sees and senses. This mind experiment helps you anticipate where the fish will be and helps you to be more stealthy when you approach them. A great way to begin is to imagine how a food source looks to a trout. Whenever I am looking at drys in a fly shop, I look at the imitation from below instead of from above. This is the view the trout will have when it is looking up to feed.

Fish like you mean it and like you'll only get one good cast for each presentation. Slow down, and always get into the best position for the best delivery. Think about, and use, all of your senses.

When searching the water, do not search for an image of the entire fish. Train yourself to scan the water for movement, shadows, or parts of the fish.

CHAPTER 3

What to Look For

To be successful at spotting fish, remember that you are not looking for a picture-perfect view of the entire fish. You are scanning the water for clues—silhouette, motion, shadow, the wink of a white mouth, color. As soon as you banish the image of an entire fish from your head, you will spot more of them. Confidence comes with practice. One of the first things to do is to watch a lot of fish and pick up on all the clues—silhouette, motion, and shadow, for instance—that give it away. As you teach yourself what to look for, don't be afraid to spook some fish. Learn from what you see and use that information to spot fish in the rest of the water.

Beginning sight-fishing anglers make the mistake of looking for the entire fish. I always emphasize that they should look for anything that seems out of place, such as a silhouette, a white mouth opening, or a fish's markings. However, clues can be even more subtle than that. Sometimes, especially in deep and dirty water or in cloudy weather, all you see is a small portion of the trout's body.

In clear water, all the clues for spotting trout—from seeing the opening of the trout's mouth to the shadow it casts on the river bottom—are visible. Though dirty water makes it harder to spot fish, it is not impossible, as long as you have some visibility—even if it is only one foot past the surface. This is when trout feed best: stained water provides plenty of cover, allowing fish to gorge without worry.

Silhouettes

The first thing I look for is the silhouette or ghostlike image of a trout. This is a vague hue, even a translucent color—it sometimes looks like an illusion or feels like your eyes are playing tricks on you.

23

Sometimes you'll only spot a flash of color or small part of the trout's body. In this photo, the water is dirty after a heavy rain, and only the trout's tail is visible.

In many situations, especially in deep water, you will only see the ghostly blue image of a trout.

In some cases, the silhouette is something that seems unnatural—the vague shape of a trout in the river, not an outline of a fish. This is especially true in deep, colored, or stained water. The deeper it goes in dirty water, the more a fish blends in with its surroundings. Sometimes the only visible part of its body is its back, which can be almost identical to the color of the water.

To help my clients understand what I mean by a ghostly image, I ask them first to imagine a painting with a dark outline filled in with color or shading. This would be similar to seeing the outline of the trout in the water when you can see the body and fins of the fish. Now imagine a watercolor painting of a fish without an outline, painted in light pastel colors. This is what the ghostly image of a fish looks like.

Movement

After finding a silhouette, the next step is to detect any movement made by the image to determine if what you are looking at is indeed a trout. We will talk about reading these different types of movement in chapter 8, but the main thing to understand here is that movement—any movement—is a clue. Even if a trout is feeding by simply sipping in an insect, it will always have a part of its body in motion to hold its position, most notably its pectoral and tail fins, which keep it stationary.

In clear water, it is generally not that difficult to discern a trout, but it is quite a challenge if there is any stain to the water. Sometimes all you see is a slight half-inch movement of the tail or dorsal fin. These two parts of the trout's body constantly give me a confirmed sighting because they are the closest to the water's surface.

In addition to fin movement, the most obvious way to detect a trout is from body movements, whether those movements are up-and-down while suspended in a run or side-to-side in shallow water. These movements tell you more about the behavior of the trout and where it is feeding,

which allows you to make more accurate presentations. Watch for signs that the trout is opening its mouth to take in food. This tells you exactly where to drift the flies.

The food that fish eat, whether on the surface or subsurface, is constantly moving in the river's currents, and so is the trout as it intercepts its food. Understanding this is helpful when you need to distinguish between a piece of vegetation swaying in the current or a trout. Sticks and weeds move the same all the time and don't change positions. The trout's movements will never be repetitive.

I also watch the river bottom. For example, if I think I see a trout holding in a run near some vegetation, I watch the movement of the growth on the river bottom and then focus back on the silhouette. A trout will look like it is hovering in the water with more controlled movement. Vegetation is anchored and has a snakelike movement.

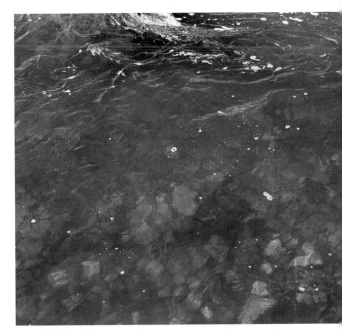

Fins and tails are two of the most common clues to look for. This photo shows a common tail image of a brown trout holding next to structure where it can escape if it spooks from the feeding lane it is holding in.

Trout love to hug the banks while feeding, because cover is nearby. These photos show the trout as if you were standing on the river's edge, looking into the water. Can you spot the fish?

The circle reveals the hidden trout (mouth closed).

The same fish has its mouth open in this photo.

The circle reveals the open-mouthed trout.

Shadows

A fish's shadow on the bottom of the river betrays the fish's position, and indicates that it is suspended off the bottom. Generally, fish that are suspended (as opposed to hugging the bottom) are likely to take your fly. Even if the shadow is distorted because of turbulent water, it is an excellent clue in varying water and weather conditions because it looks different from anything else on the river bottom, no matter what conditions you are fishing in. Many objects can look like a shadow on the river bottom, especially in deep water, but a trout's shadow is usually darker than the vegetation or other objects, and it will move more.

It might seem obvious, but it is nonetheless worth stating that a fish's shadow is more apparent in sunny conditions. The same sun can cast shadows that betray your presence to the fish. Be mindful not only of your shadow, but also the shadows from your line.

The White Glint

The inside of every trout's mouth is bright white or pastel pink. Spotting a white mouth has saved the day for me onstream many times. In dirty or

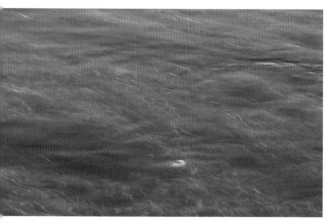

In dirty water, the best indicator of a trout actively feeding is seeing its open mouth.

stained water where silhouettes and colors are not visible, the flash of the trout's mouth tells you that there is an actively feeding fish in the water.

A fish opens its mouth not only to breathe, but also to feed. The challenge is knowing when the trout is feeding and not just breathing. If the fish opens its mouth without moving, it is probably just breathing. And when a trout opens its mouth constantly without noticeable pause or pattern, it is usually breathing. When trout do feed, the opening is aggressive and often larger than when it breathes because the fish has to aggressively close down on a food source to consume it. In addition to the movements of the trout's mouth, observe its feeding pattern. When a trout feeds, there are usually resting periods in between each take. When it is breathing, it constantly moves its mouth.

Cracking the Color Code

In spring 2008, Colorado had some of the roughest cold weather conditions in recent history, with water fluctuating on a regular basis. Finding trout in areas where they could find shelter was a challenge because they were spread out so much. The dirty water from slow snowmelt caused the water to remain the color of pea soup for weeks. The search for small dorsal fins or the red cheeks of a rainbow became critical.

I had a client named Rob Bouwens, whose passion and love for the sport could be felt from a mile away. He sure had Zen. Before we left on our trip, whether we said it or not, we were both concerned with the low water conditions. After a few hours of hiking around the river, we came to a run that usually held fish, but it was very dirty.

Rob drifted repeatedly through the run with no results. I saw a small red object that I think even an eagle would have mistaken for a rock. I quickly asked Rob to hold tight and wait a minute while I scanned the section of water. That red dot, the size of a nickel, would occasionally appear. I patiently waited, and fifteen minutes later, I spotted the large,

Rainbows are colorful; their lateral lines and gill plates are marked with gorgeous colors. It is the back of the trout that allows it to blend in, especially in deep water. This trout would disappear in a deep, dark green run.

Rob Bouwens takes the time for a quick lift and picture before a quick release of the prize catch of the day.

white opening of a 'bow's mouth. After some fine-tuning and some correct presentations with me peering over Rob's shoulder, the mouth opened and the trout took. The violent head shakes to the surface with line-ripping runs ended when he landed a flawless male 'bow.

I always get a kick out of looking at photos I have taken of clients holding a brightly colored fish. I often think to myself, "We almost walked right past that beauty." Coloration can be deceiving when it comes to seeing trout in the water. This is due to the refraction of light when you are trying to see trout below the water's surface.

Refraction is when the water bends or distorts the light and images below the surface. For example, when viewing a fish at a 45-degree angle, refraction makes it appear as if you were looking at it from a 32-degree angle. This is why the major-

ity of what you see of a trout's body is the back or lateral line and not the whole side of the fish.

Most of the time you are looking down at the trout below the water at this 45-degree angle. This view is deceiving because what you see below the water's surface is angled differently and distorted. To see an example of this phenomenon, fill a glass half-full of water and put a pencil in it. The pencil looks like it bends in the water and becomes larger than the actual size of the pencil out of the water.

Most of what you see of the trout is at this 32-degree angle. This puts the back and lateral line of the trout in main view. For example, rainbow trout have spots along the lateral line and backs that resemble the blue and green colors in a deep run. These camouflaged markings and the light refraction hide the fish; you can

Brightly colored rainbows have red lateral lines, which are more noticeable when you are looking at the upper part of the trout's body from a 45-degree angle.

spot them easier when you see the pastel red markings along the lateral line and the gill plate. This is why many rainbows pod up during migration periods when the visible markings along their laterals are less noticeable. The trout move

in numbers for safety, unlike browns, which are more independent.

When the lower side or belly of the trout is disguised, a fish's color is hard to see. For instance, a brown trout has a back that matches the river bottom, and the lateral line is speckled with black spots that look like cracks in the rocks. The bright, vibrant colors of the belly are difficult to see.

The size of the trout also appears to change in different water depths. The deeper the trout is in the river, the larger the image will appear, but the colors stand out more. The shallower the water, the smaller the image will appear. In shallow water you have fewer opportunities to see more of the trout's body.

Every trout has its own beautiful, unique markings. Some are more visible than others, but they all help you to determine what species you see. Each trout has distinct features that give it away in the water. That is why I personally enjoy hunting trout more than any sport fish; no two fish have the same markings, even in the same species. The following list describes the different colors or markings you should look for.

Brown trout are some of the hardest trout to see because most of their color is on the belly. Their lateral lines are riddled with black, brown, and red spots, which resemble cracks in the rocks on the river bottom.

Even the brightest colored trout can be difficult to see, especially in low light.

This brown trout with its camouflaged colors all but disappears in these low-light conditions.

Cutthroat have orange gill plates, fins, and bellies, making them one of the easiest species to spot. Eric Koehler watched this fish take his fly.

Some rainbows have brilliant red sides, but these colors are not always easy to see in shallow, riffley water.

Rainbows/Cuttbows

The markings of rainbow trout, or cuttbows, are generally more obvious to anglers than other species because most of the color is along their lateral lines and gill plates, which are the parts most visible to anglers. The color ranges from bright red to pastel purple.

Although they are usually easier to see, this is not the case if the river bottom is covered with different colored rocks of green, blue, or red. Also, in the spring when the rainbows and cuttbows are in prespawn mode, their markings are subtle and the gill plates and lateral lines are a light pastel color instead of vibrant reds.

This is when you should look for the brightness of the trout as a target. Because large trout in the spring come from big bodies of deep water, they do not need the colors to match the river bottom. Instead these trout have chrome or bright bodies, and they stand out against darker river bottoms.

Cutthroat

The many species of cutthroat have beautiful, bright coloration and markings, which make them some of the easiest trout to spot. Their markings span the whole body (including above the lateral line), so they are more visible when you are looking at them from a 45-degree angle.

Look for the bright orange gill plate, a yellow or copper colored body (some with big, dispersed spots and others finely speckled), and the distinct orange line just below the lower jaw that resembles a cut. Sometimes the colors are so bright that the orange will bleed into red. While this gives you an advantage when you are looking for them in the water, it is during the close encounter after landing these fish when you really appreciate their true beauty. Without question, the cutthroat is one of the most beautifully colored trout in the world.

Brown trout

Because most of a brown trout's colors are on the belly and fins, they are the hardest to spot. Above the lateral line are black and brown spots on an olive or brown back, making the fish seem to melt into the river bottom. Unlike the rainbow and cutthroat trout, the browns tend to travel alone when they inhabit a river, so you have to be on full alert, because there are fewer of them to see.

I focus on the olive or brown back of the fish, which is darker than other species, and on their large, bright fins. Unlike other trout, browns, especially the larger browns, are long and lean with unusually large fins. When the bright orange and yellow fins are moving, they are easy to spot. With the male's large head and long, extended body and fins, a brown resembles the shape of an alliga-

Brown trout closely match the river bottom. Their unusually large fins often give away their location.

tor in the water. Look also for the color differences of the fins: this varies depending on where they live, or the species of brown. In the West, many browns have orange and yellow translucent fins that are visible in clear water when the sun penetrates through the fins. In the East, many browns have black fins, which stand out in different river conditions.

Brook trout

Brook trout live in clear, high-mountain streams and lakes. These fish have some of the most brilliant and distinguishable colors. Their backs are a light and dark olive pattern that looks to me like ground beef, though the technical term is vermiculation. There are pink spots surrounded by bright blue haloes along the lateral line. However, the true sign that you have spotted a brookie is the bright, light color of the belly that extends onto the fins. Every brook trout has a white stripe down the front of the bottom fin. Brookies often live in stained water, but even in stained water, this white stripe is a dead giveaway.

Brook trout have some of the most breathtaking markings, reminding anglers why they pursue this great fish. The brush-filled waters where these brightly colored trout live make it hard for predators to reach them. JACK HANRAHAN

Watch for migrating trout just as the sun begins to rise, and right before sunset. You can easily spot trout in shallow side channels and skinny water.

CHAPTER 4

Body Language

Not every trout you spot is willing to take a fly. Understanding the fish's behavior by reading its movements helps you determine if the trout you see is a feeding fish or one that should be passed by. This, admittedly, can be hard to do, but learning to leave uninterested fish alone will serve you well in the end because you can focus more time and effort on willing fish. Once you have found a willing target, pay attention to the fish's movements: that will let you know if it has taken your fly (the fish is always the best strike indicator), if it has refused the fly, or if it has spooked. Then modify your approach accordingly.

Because fish are cold-blooded, water temperature plays a critical role in the amount that a trout moves. Water temperatures below 40 degrees and above 65 degrees slow fish down. In warm water or extremely cold water, trout are lethargic and may only move a few inches to take a fly. However, trout do adapt to different rivers and waterways throughout the world. For instance, tailwater trout are more accustomed to cold temperatures than trout that live in rivers with wide temperature fluctuations. When temperatures are ideal, and the food source warrants it, fish will move many feet. That's when your odds of hooking a trout are good because the trout is solely concentrating on the food, and they are not as wary of predators from above.

Rainbows, cutthroats, and cuttbows are more active, in my opinion, when water temperatures are on the rise. On the other hand, brown and brook trout seem to be more active when the temperature drops. This is related to feeding behavior and migrating behavior. For instance, in the spring, after water temperatures have been in the 40-degree range during the winter, the days grow longer and the temperatures begin to increase: rainbows, cutthroats, and cuttbows become more active as they begin to migrate before spawning.

Large trout are often easy to spot. When this huge brown turned sideways to eat a mayfly nymph it caused a swirl on the water's surface with its broad shoulders.

In the fall, as the warm temperatures of summer begin to drop to the low 50s or high 40s, the browns and brook trout begin their migration in preparation to spawn.

Feeding Fish

Feeding fish are prime targets and part of what makes sight fishing so exciting. When you first spot a trout in a run, determine how deep the fish

A brown trout explodes on a caddis from ten feet away. It is a rush to watch a trout chase its food. ANGUS DRUMMOND

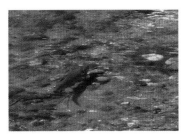 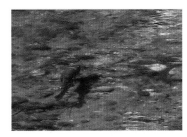 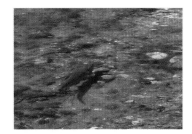

When a trout moves to its side to eat your fly, wait for it to straighten out after the turn. This will ensure that the trout has opened and closed its mouth on the fly before you set, preventing you from setting too early.

is holding below the surface. Fish feeding on the surface, at least in relatively calm water, are easy to spot by the riseforms that they make and their position high in the water column.

I have become a believer over the years that a suspended fish is a feeding fish, at least most of the time. Fish hold in three areas: top column, midcolumn, and hugging the bottom. While trout can feed anywhere, fish holding in the midcolumn or just below the surface in the top column are more willing to take the fly. When a trout is hugging the bottom, it can and will feed, but this is also where trout rest and therefore are less active.

The biggest indication that a fish is feeding subsurface is the flash of a white mouth, which sometimes looks like an underwater glint. I see this only 60 percent of the time. (I talk more about this in chapter 3). Fish also open their mouths to breathe, but when they open their mouths to eat, they are usually also moving. An eating fish extends its mouth more when it feeds than it would when it is breathing, and the white glint is more apparent. Timing is also different. When a fish is breathing, it constantly opens and closes its mouth to consume oxygen. When it is feeding, there is typically a pattern, with longer pauses between each opening.

In dirtier water, riffles, or high water, when you cannot see the white mouth, look for the fish's silhouette moving in one of three ways: up and down, side to side, or chasing—all following some

sort of drift. When a fish feeds it will drift back to look at its food, to investigate it before it eats.

When a fish moves to get into the same plane as the food, the current pushes it backward. This is more apparent when a fish takes food off the top of the water. When its body tilts to look up, the water pushes it back farther. When eating subsurface food, the trout's body will not tilt upward as much, causing less drift. A fish can move up and down by simply flipping its pectoral fins up or down to tilt its body in the direction of its food, which lets the current push it toward its next move. This rise-and-fall feeding motion is common with trout holding in deeper water.

The second and probably most common movement of a feeding trout is the side-to-side movement, though trout also move this way when they spook. When a trout does feed while moving side to side, it opens its mouth on the turn toward its meal and then straightens out aggressively once it has captured its meal and closed its mouth. Then it immediately returns to its original holding position, which is a giveaway that the trout is actively feeding. When you see a white mouth in combination with this movement, you are in business.

In ideal temperatures and with ample food, trout will move a number of feet and then make a U-turn to take a fly. This aggressive feeding is without question some of the most exciting subsurface sight fishing. The fish sees a food source that has passed by its viewing lane, or is drifting some feet away, and it turns downstream ahead of the food source; it makes a quick U-turn when it is below the insect, opens its mouth, and viciously takes the fly. Trout that feed in this way are willing to chase their food, and you do not have to be on

We spotted this trout by its regular flashing, like a strobe. The challenge was determining if the fish flashed for our fly or for a natural.

Pete Kolasa saw this brown nestled between two rocks, actively feeding deep in a run. Because there were rocks on both sides of where the trout was holding, it would not spook when approached correctly, resulting in a cool visual take in clear water.

point with every cast. I have seen trout swim fifteen to twenty feet to turn and take a fly.

Trout (and other species) get excited when they spot a meal. A trout will flare its fins and the dorsal fin will stand straight up, steadying its body in the river. It always reminds me of a dorado when it spots a baitfish and flares its fins and lights up. In clear or slack water where you can see all of a trout's fins, this can be your best clue as to whether the trout is actively feeding—and if it is getting ready to pounce on your fly.

In dark, dirty water or low light, look for the flash of a feeding fish as it turns to eat a meal. While it only lasts a brief second, a flash lets you know there is an active trout in the water. The flash not only tells you where the trout is, but depending on the number and frequency of flashes, you can determine if the trout is actively feeding, or only occasionally taking a meal when it drifts by. The flash lets you know where the fish is feeding—for instance, eating nymphs on the bottom of a run or consuming an emerging insect a foot or inches below the surface of the water.

Subsurface flashes can also be whitefish or other silvery fish, so it is important to look for spots or the shape of the tail in addition to the flash. Also, whitefish and dace concentrate in great numbers in deep runs, and when they are actively feeding you will see numerous flashes that look identical in that deep section of water.

One of the disadvantages of sight fishing to a feeding fish, and using its feeding motions as an indication of when to strike, is that many anglers become strike-happy, and set anytime the fish moves. But it is absolutely critical to follow the path of your flies, try to anticipate where they are at all times, and only set when you see an indication that the fish has fed and your fly is in front of the fish. This is important because if you constantly set the hook with split shot and tandem rigs, you run a high risk of foul-hooking fish or scaring fish because you are moving your flies so much.

Many guides teach anglers to set the hook anytime they see the fish move (or anytime the indicator moves, which can be worse), but I prefer to coach people to know where their flies are at all times and set the hook when they see the fish open its mouth or make a feeding motion. But fish move for a lot of reasons other than feeding, so this is an important clarification.

When a fish takes a fly, it immediately moves its head (a head shake) to relieve the pressure. By immediately, I mean that this will generally happen before your strike indicator even moves. Because of this, I often tell my clients who are setting the hook too early to wait until they see the head shake. In challenging visibility, I may have to walk my clients through the presentation and hookup because they are unable to spot the fish. I watch the fish move for their fly, and if I am not sure that the fish has eaten the fly, I wait for the head shake (that occurs almost instantly) before I tell them to set. This, more often than not, results in a fair hookup.

This is why thinking short is important (see chapter 10 on presentation). If the fish does not

Steve Henderson could not fool a fish until the sun dropped. At high noon when the fish's and angler's visibility were both good, the trout would simply move out of the way of the rig.

turn on the fly to eat it, the flies drift by the fish. Accurate presentations are critical.

"Hook set" is a misnomer, in my opinion. Because of the tension on the leader from the current, and the fish turning on the fly, the hook is already penetrating the fish's mouth—by lifting the rod, you are merely *ensuring* the placement and driving it deeper. As soon as the fish feels tension, it will shake its head, which is a sure indicator that you should lift the rod. As this happens, there is some movement in the leader, indicator, or fly line, though it can be extremely subtle.

There are times when a trout will suck in the fly and blow it out extremely fast, without the fly penetrating its jaw. I see this a lot when fishing an egg imitation, because the round material on the egg reduces the hook gap, making it easier for the fish to spit out the fly. When you can see the trout spit out the fly, you have a clear view of the fish. Then you have to react by setting fast to ensure the penetration of the hook, but remember that you can set quickly by lifting without overpowering the rod and causing the tippet material to break.

Spooked Fish

The best sight anglers in the world are the ones who know when to call it quits and move on to another target. That means that you need to be able to spot a spooked or nervous fish. A dead giveaway that you have spooked a fish is when you see it swim quickly up or downstream. There is nothing slow or lazy about its movements—the fish will be traveling fast. It is most likely heading to its retreat spot (under a rock, under a stream bank, to the turbulent water at the head of the pool), and it will be in a hurry. Ignore these fish until they have the chance to settle down again.

Another more subtle sign of a spooked fish is a trout slowly changing its position. It can be a fish that slowly and deliberately sinks lower in the water to be closer to the bottom, or one that slowly swims farther away from you as you approach it. Spooked fish sometimes just move out of the way as your rig goes by them. When a trout does move out of the way of your imitation, it will typically not return to the original position because that section of water is now a threat. One of

the most deceptive movements a trout will make in a run while your flies are drifting downstream is a sideways movement to get out of the way of the unnatural object in the river. I see this a lot when a trout has detected split shot on a nymph rig. It looks like a sideways movement to eat a fly, but the trout is simply avoiding any contact with the object in the water. When this occurs, the fish often will not return to the position in which it was holding when you spotted it. Sometimes the fish will appear as if it is investigating your pattern, but it is really trying to get out of the way. Determining if the trout is interested in feeding or just trying to avoid contact with your flies or rig is a huge part of choosing a target that is worth pursuing. If its movements are wary, the trout is spooked. Adjust your drift or rig to look more natural, or continue your journey in pursuit of a worthy customer.

Another way to tell if the fish is nervous is by a change in its feeding pattern. When you spot a feeding fish, observe it over a period of time to determine how it is feeding: erratically, steadily, at what rate, or only that one time. Once you have this frame of reference, and you have spotted a fish that is feeding regularly every five seconds, any deviation from that baseline can indicate that the fish has spooked.

Holding Still

Fish that are holding still are often not feeding, though they are worth a look. I see a lot of fish holding still in riffles and deep water, hugging the bottom. Since riffles are prime feeding areas, if I see a fish holding still in the riffles, I wait before making a cast. I watch the trout's behavior to see if

Facing page: Watching a trophy fish take your fly like a natural will forever change how you fish. Mike Deherrera became a believer in sight fishing after landing this fish of a lifetime.

This brown was fooled in low water by a different approach from the earlier days' fishing. A dark streamer in deep holding water was just the right approach.

it is lying still or pausing between feeding. If the trout is lying still it is likely nervous, or not a target worth pursuing aggressively. If a fish is in the riffles, just holding, it could be sickly—perhaps it was just released by another angler twenty minutes ago and is recuperating, or it could be warming in the shallower water but not feeding.

If it is not feeding, if it's in an atypical spot, or if it does not have much cover, I might make a few casts, but if the fish doesn't react to the flies I definitely won't spend too much time on it. If I do cast to it, I cast short to keep the flies on the side closest to me so that the fish moves to take the fly. This is the worst setup for lining a fish: if you do not cast short and the trout is not feeding, the flies will drift into the trout, resulting in a spooked or foul-hooked trout.

In deep water, a fish that is holding on the bottom may not be actively feeding, but I like this setup. The fish has ample cover because of the water depth, making it feel more secure. Since the fish has a wide angle of view, I can adjust my rig, starting higher in the water and working down closer to the fish to entice it to eat.

Migrating Fish

In the spring and fall, you may see fish swimming through shallow riffles or porpoising as they migrate to their spawning grounds. I often see trout on my home waters of the South Platte, porpoising like dolphins as the light falls in the evening. This is a good indication that there are fresh fish moving upstream. On the East Coast's Great Lakes, the brown trout and steelhead migrate in huge numbers, and the fish are large. When the fish move into the tributaries of the lakes, their backs are out of the water in shallow runs while they fight their way upstream.

A migrating fish generally travels early or late in the day and will be willing to move through water so shallow that it will have its back out of the water. But this stresses the fish. They are more likely to eat your fly once they reach deeper water. Wakes in deep water moving upstream, especially in the evening, are often signs of migratory fish.

Don't cast to moving fish. Wait until they stop and stage before making a presentation. You can ambush these fish at prime holding areas where they stop. Fish smarter by picking areas where you can get a good presentation and where the fish are easiest to see.

Territorial Fish

Prespawn fish can be territorial—males chase other males. They can also be territorial year-round about positioning in the stream. The biggest indication of this is aggressive behavior. I frequently see large trout holding in the "A" position at the head of a run, where a shallow riffle flows into it. The fish chases off other fish. Since this is the best spot in the run to consume food, it is occupied by the baddest fish. It is also a prime spot to stage before fish spawn, so it is the arena for lots of prespawn aggression. When trout are territorial, they move sporadically, so they become difficult to cast to. They concentrate on defending their territory and attacking anything that challenges them, making nymphs and dry flies unproductive. Streamers appear to be a challenge to the territorial trout and can trigger an aggressive take.

A good example is an encounter I had last year with my good friend Angus Drummond as we were walking along the Dream Stream, covering miles of water in the hunt for a big brown. To our surprise, after three hours of hiking without a brown in sight, we stumbled upon six large male browns that were fighting for territory in a long, slow, deep run. They were all around the same size, about 6 to 8 pounds. We looked at each other and thought, "Game on!" After pursuing the fish with dry flies, streamers, nymphs, and pretty much everything we had in our boxes, it was apparent that these fish were there to fight for rights—even a decent size streamer was not enough to entice a strike.

Later that night at home I reflected on the fishes' aggressive behavior and how I could get one of them to slam a fly. Then it came to me: I needed to think big—really big. Fortunately, I had a guide trip the following day with John Wexler, a well-traveled angler who had many saltwater patterns that I hoped would be big enough for the task.

The next day we arrived on the water early. Sure enough, four of the big fish were still there, fighting for the water. The largest brown in the bunch was our target. We pulled out a 9-inch-long Puglisi baitfish with an olive back and chrome sides, which might imitate a baby rainbow trout. After we rigged, I thought, "Here goes nothing," and we ducked to prevent getting hit with the monster fly. It landed on the water four feet above the pod of fish. John stripped, and *Wham!* The big brown smashed the fly. After a battle, we brought the 8 1/2-pound male to the net. We would not have caught it if we had tried a different approach.

Foam lines are magnets for fish because they concentrate food. Above, an angler casts to a pod of rising trout in a giant foam line. When indicator fishing, use a white indicator that blends in with the foam.

CHAPTER 5

Uncovering the Trout

If you want to buy a baseball bat for one of your kids, the first thing you do is to go to a sporting goods store. You wouldn't waste your time in a specialty golf store. Similarly, sight fishing for trout starts with reading the water by looking into areas where trout would most likely hold: don't waste time looking in unproductive water. Reading the water is important; in sight fishing it is a means to an end. You use your reading skills to find targets, rather than just fishing the water with the faith that trout are there.

Keep things simple so you don't get overwhelmed wondering where to start looking for trout. To simplify my search, I think about the three things that trout need to survive: cover, oxygen, and a food supply. If a piece of water has one or more of these, I start looking closely. The best places to sight-fish have several of these requirements and good visibility.

Oxygen and food are incredibly important; fish will leave the safety of cover for oxygen or food. But in this chapter, I am going to focus on some other sources of cover that trout seek and explain what I look for to see them better.

Fish are alert for natural predators, and fishing pressure makes them wary. Security is a top priority for fish when choosing where to hold and feed. The biggest challenge in sight fishing is to not spook the trout and to let the fish remain stress-free in the cover it found. Cover can be anything from deep water, structure, shadows, or broken surface currents. Fish may leave the security of the cover to feed or migrate, but this puts them increasingly on edge—unless they are feeding so gluttonously that they only pay attention to the food. Cover is the first place to start looking.

Structure supplies great seams and areas in which trout will hold. ANGUS DRUMMOND

Snowy, cloud-filled skies make trout of all sizes comfortable, and if you can brave the elements, you'll be rewarded. FRANK MARTIN

I will describe some places where I regularly look for fish. Time after time, these areas produce well for me, so I confidently search there for fish, even in rivers new to me. When I am out fishing, or guiding my clients into fish, I first identify the prime area, look for a viewing lane or window, and then watch for a fish's movements.

After I describe the area, I will describe the viewing windows that are common in each. A viewing window is a small opening on the surface of the water that allows you to see through an otherwise hard-to-see area—slicks in turbulent water, open water in pockets of vegetation, patches of light on the bottom of an otherwise dark-bottom stream.

Rocks

The first spots I target in waters with structure are rocks or log jams. These areas create a cushion of washed-out river bottom that makes the trout feel safe. Moreover, the water speeds up before break-

This viewing window through structure gives you a view of the trout so that you can investigate its feeding activity before you make a presentation. These windows are great locations to study trout behavior while you stay out of view in the safety of the structure at the river's edge.

A brown trout felt secure under this seam, and it fed without worry.

Trout can hold on all sides of large rocks, making them excellent cover. Don't forget to look for trout in front of the rocks.

ing over the structure, reducing the trout's time to investigate the flies.

As the current flows around rocks, it creates prime seams in which fish feed. These seams provide cover because the water disturbance helps hide the fish. Fish hold there and the food is delivered right to them on either side of the fast water, ideal for a trout because it does not have to expend energy to eat.

Without rocks for structure, trout would not be able to hold in many of the small waterways throughout the United States. In areas without rocks, such as smooth-running sand bottoms on spring creeks, trout are more wary. I grew up fishing the Dream Stream with the only structure close to the dam on the upper half of the five-and-a-half-mile stretch. This supplied great, long-running, deep, and riffled runs, prime for summertime bug activity. It was difficult for the fish to find cover in such clear water. Over the last twenty years, man-made rock improvements were added to more than half of this section of water to pre-vent erosion. Now there are areas for trout to hold, including large migratory fish in the numbers and sizes we had not seen before. Rocks are important holding spots for trout so that they can remain wary, free, and healthy.

Most anglers fish the pools and runs and they overlook pocketwater because it can be challenging to fish. One way to find private water on a public river is to fish where others won't. Pat Dorsey searches a great pocket run in Cheesman Canyon.

The window

Many anglers ignore the cushions created in front of rocks, so I often feel like they are my secret spots. The current washes out a pocket in front of the structure, which gives the trout a spot to hold and feed. The structure also causes a break in the surface of the water, giving you a clear view of the fish. There is a window behind structure as well, a slow portion of water created when the two seams break to flow around the object.

Pocketwater

Pocketwater not only provides cover in the form of rocks, but it also has fast water. In general, anglers fish pocketwater less because it is not easy to get to and wade around in, and the complex seams make drifts difficult. Pat Dorsey says, "One of the most overlooked components of a trout stream is fishing fast, oxygenated pocketwater. Many anglers avoid pocketwater because it is extremely difficult to negotiate. This can be a huge

oversight, however, especially during post-runoff periods because all the 'hard-to-get-to places' that were buried during the high-water season now hold good numbers of trout with the highly-oxygenated currents, ideal water temperatures, abundant hatches, and good holding water.

"Targeting the tough-to-get-to areas has always been a secret of my trade. I frequently use a wading staff in pocketwater to ensure good footing, because these swift pieces of water are slick and difficult to maneuver. Due to the lack of pressure, trout eagerly rise to dry flies in calm pockets and readily take dead-drifted nymphs in the fast-flowing seams.

"Dry/droppers are especially effective in these areas. I typically fish a size 14 to 16 Rubber-Legged Stimulator with a size 18 to 20 Tungsten Flashback Pheasant Tail or a size 20 Mercer's Tungsten Micro Mayfly. I will dap the dry/dropper rig into the pocket and carefully watch for trout to dart out and grab the dry fly or dropper fly. I also nymph these areas with a standard two-fly nymphing rig using both short-line (high-sticking) and long-line strategies, which help to extend my drift in the mini-pool created by the boulder. Good line management is critical for success in pocketwater; it helps avoid conflicting currents and drag, which often result in a poor presentation. I frequently find myself fishing straight upriver, which helps me avoid these tricky currents.

"Anglers should always be on the prowl looking for suspended trout—telltale signs the trout are actually feeding—in front of rocks, in the glassy part of the pocket, or in the seams. Anglers must have a keen eye to be successful in pocketwater. Savvy anglers cover the water methodically, showing their flies to as many trout as possible. Cover every nook and cranny. Anglers need to focus on what goes on around their strike indicator (dry fly) rather than focusing strictly on their strike indicator or dry fly. Any type of movement in the water column is a sure sign a trout has taken your fly and the hook should be set immediately."

Pat Dorsey displays one of many gems found on the South Platte.

In turbulent water, these slick-water windows are great places to scan the river's bottom, where trout feel safe and feed without interruption. Scan through these windows with unfocused eyes as they drift downstream, and you will be rewarded with a view of the river bottom.

The window

You can find windows in front of and behind rocks in pocketwater stretches, but you should also look for smooth, glasslike breaks in the disturbance of fast water. These windows move downstream, so once you find one, you must follow it. Some windows are large, others are small. They might appear on a regular basis with constant breaks in the turbulent water, while others drift by sporadically. Even if you see only a fin when it drifts by, this is enough to let you know a trout is there. You can find these pocketwater windows in shallow water as well: a riffled run often has impressions that are deeper than the surrounding water, where the riffles on the water's surface disappear and provide a flat spot or window through which you can see the stream bottom.

In wood-choked streams, trout feel secure and feed with abandon—the challenge is in the presentation and the fight.

Wood

Wood in the water, whether there by natural means or placed by man, attracts fish. The water breaks around it in so many different ways that the fish find easy cover. These wooded breaks in the river also provide cover that allow fish to feed more heavily. Scum lines from foam that accumulates in front of or around the wooded objects in turbulent water supply additional cover. Tree limbs or roots that extend into the river are great feeding zones. Though presentations can be challenging (I have lost many flies around downed trees), once you find the right presentation, those fish are stress-free and are willing to move from the wooded structure to eat.

Keep things simple so that you don't get overwhelmed wondering where to start looking for trout. I always think about the three things that trout need to survive: cover, oxygen, and a food supply. JAY NICHOLS

In this stretch, foam lines and shadows provide ideal cover for trout to feed on hatching insects.

The window

The best windows will be in front or below the wood, and trout often lie on the edge of the solid, non-moving structure. Use openings in the wood to give you a view of the trout feeding below. The best windows are the ones that allow you to make a snag-free drift to the fish. If you can clearly see a trout feeding in a window but the risk of snagging the structure is too high, rethink the approach or find a new target.

Foam Lines

One of my favorite areas to find fish, partially because they are overlooked, are foam lines that provide cover and food for trout. Always investigate around and below every foam line or clump you encounter. These are great areas to sight-fish because you can get so close to the trout without it seeing you.

The window

When you are trying to spot a fish in this mess of bubbles, look for a slight opening or a portion of the foam that moves from one side of the river. The best time to fish a foam line is when the trout are feeding on adults on the top or emergers just below the surface—the dark heads and backs are a dead giveaway, especially in sunny conditions when the sun glistens off the exposed portion of their bodies. If you can't see fish in the foam, concentrate on the foam's perimeter. Trout feel safe under foam and will commonly break cover, allowing you to see them for a second.

Some of the best foam lines are the ones that do not allow you to see into them from above. Instead, you may see a tail sticking out of the back of the clump of foam.

During the late summer or early fall, when brown trout are staging or migrating in a river system, they find refuge in weeds. In spring or early summer most rivers have minimal vegetation. While it is difficult to see the trout in these vegetation-covered holding areas, the fish are happy and willing to take a fly.

Vegetation

Trout also find cover under or around vegetation. Plants are full of great food—insects and crustaceans like scuds reside here—and the trout wait there safely and find protein. It is sometimes impossible to fish in these areas without getting salad on your flies, so these spots have less angling pressure. Some of the largest trout I have ever seen were in thick green areas: underneath a lot of vegetated water is clear, clean water for trout to hold in, and they may remain undetected for weeks. The vegetation acts like a filter, which is why the water below is so clear.

Vegetation can be a problem for many anglers, but it plays an important role in supplying oxygen to the fish. As long as sunlight penetrates the water, the plants create oxygen. In slow-moving water, trout hide or reside in vegetation-filled areas of the river, not just for food supply but also for the good

supply of oxygen. This occurs a lot in late summer and early fall when the vegetation in rivers has grown to its full potential. Vegetated areas are often holding grounds for trout in the early morning or late evening. The fish move away from the vegetation when the water temperatures are cool in late fall, winter, and early spring, or when a supply of food is abundant.

The window

As the year progresses, the amount of vegetation along the river bottom increases tremendously, especially in nutrient-rich tailwaters and spring creeks where the sun penetrates the clear water easily. Weedy areas in a river are ideal holding and feeding places for trout, but they can be a nightmare to fish. Not only can the fish tuck up under the weeds, making them impossible to spot, but every time you try to get a drift, it seems like you hang up on the weeds. However, pockets in the

In this photo, the clear pocket of water in a weed-filled run is a prime area for trout to move into and feed when they emerge from the cover of weeds.

Trout holding on the edge of the river demand incredibly slow and careful approaches so that you can get into casting position without spooking them.

vegetation that are clear of weeds provide a clear view of the trout as well as an opening to drift your fly into without snagging weeds. Cast to the top of the opening in the weeds, drift through the weedless water, and then recast before you snag.

Weedy areas often hold large fish, and I can't pass them up even if there are no pockets. I fish a streamer near the vegetation in hopes of luring a fish out and getting a reaction strike. Cast far across the section of water you are fishing, and

Undercut banks provide cover. Since it is hard to present a fly to a fish that is holding under the bank, find a trout that has come out of hiding in search of food.

then use the fastest retrieve possible to get a trout to lift up from the vegetation, giving away its position. Once you know the trout's position, you at least have something to target.

Edges and Banks

Edges are overlooked areas for two reasons: 1) getting a correct drift in the slower water is extremely challenging, and 2) wading right into the water spooks the trout. Fish feel comfortable here because they have cover if they need to escape and tuck right next to the edge of the bank. In addition, they usually don't have to battle water flows. I love these areas because of the challenging drift—and because most of the trout holding on the edges are large.

Washed-out, undercut banks are great cover for trout. They'll dwell in these areas completely undetected, moving out to feed and racing back under them when they spook. The time to pursue them is when they move from their hideout to feed.

Back currents are often the result of a backeddy, where there is a slight cut or break in the bank, causing the water's current to swirl in a circular motion. These are great areas for trout to hold and wait for their food to be caught in the crosscurrent—and be delivered to their viewing lane. The trick is to look for a trout facing backward in these backward currents instead of looking for a trout facing upstream. Flows in eddies are slower than the main channel. This requires a stealthy approach, but provides time to watch the trout's behavior and plan the best presentation.

The window

This is one of the hardest situations to avoid spooking the trout because the water's surface is flat with little or no turbulence. However, the tradeoff is that it is fairly easy to detect movement or a silhouette if you approach from the right angle. When walking upstream looking into this

Good Timing

Timing is one of the most critical aspects of fishing. If you have good timing, you'll catch more fish. If you can be on the water during a certain season or time of day when the temperatures are ideal and supplying adequate oxygen, you'll find trout spread throughout the river, giving you more opportunities. In the dead of August, when water temperatures are at the highest, the trout will be lethargic. If you go out at 12 o'clock in the afternoon and look in your favorite spots and don't see any fish, you are not necessarily looking in the wrong areas, but your timing is off. If you get out at first light or late in the evening, the trout will be more active.

Timing is critical during seasons when temperatures are cooler, as well. Spring and fall, my favorite seasons, are times of good oxygen supply for the fish. They spread throughout the river and give you more areas to look for them. To adapt to changes in weather, water temperatures, flows, and other variables, trout swim to suitable areas to dwell and feed. If you fish only the same piece of water or the same water type, you are at a disadvantage. Remember that trout live in a wide range of habitats.

Clouds and shadows are excellent cover that give anglers an advantage because trout cannot easily see past the surface of the water. Because shadows, movement, and light reflection are not as obvious to the fish, you can get closer and make more drifts to a trout. In winter or spring, I tell my clients that powder days are better spent on the water than on the slopes because the low light triggers trout to feed, and the thick snowfall reduces and distorts the trout's visibility. The sky is dark, preventing fish from detecting the movements of dark objects, like an angler from above. Always remember that if it is easy for you to see the trout, it is easy for the trout to see you. Tough

In the summer, trout are generally more active in the morning and evening. Jim Wetherford caught this brown during a late afternoon in August.

lighting conditions provide some of the best sight fishing because the trout is less likely to detect you—but you have to train yourself to see them.

Depth is its own form of cover, even in relatively clear water. This trout is holding at the bottom of a run, safe from predators above.

flat water, look for tail movement; the downstream approach normally shows a silhouette or sideways movement when the trout eats.

In high water I look for trout hanging in tail-outs or river edges; the fish are secure there and hold in high flows without battling the current. But in flat-water scenarios, the fish have the ability to spot you better. So when you come across this water, slow down and take the time to scan it thoroughly. Try to think from the trout's perspective to understand what movements would make you most visible and threatening. Treading with caution is the trick in flat water.

Deep Water

Depth itself is a form of cover, and even if the area is only one or two feet deeper than the rest of the river, the fish will seek it. These deeper areas are the most common feeding grounds for trout. Not only do they feel safer, but food washes into a shelf

following a riffle or deep pool, the deep water is colder, and there is plenty of oxygen at the heads of runs or riffles. Trout can disappear in deep-water runs, pockets, or pools. As the water depth increases, the colors darken to deep greens or blues, helping the fish disappear—so much so that it is like reading in the dark.

High points are great areas to get a clear view of the trout, whether standing on a high bank on the river's edge or, like in this photo, hiking up to a high vantage point. You will know where you need to fish once you get an image of the trout from on high.

Riffled runs are some of the most productive areas in the river. Once a trout detects food drifting downstream in fast-moving water, it only has a split second to commit.

The window

While it would be ideal to find trout in shallow water all the time, it just is not possible. Many runs, pools, or eddies where trout love to feed are deeper than four feet, and the dark green or blue water matches the color of the fish's back. This is when a staring contest between you and the river begins. Gaze into the deep water with wide-open eyes, looking for subtle movements or outlines of the trout.

One of the easiest signs to see is the white mouth blinking as it opens and shuts. I have detected many fish in runs by the white glint when the trout opens its mouth to feed. When you do see the opening, remember the white glint will be larger than any other opening of the fish's mouth while it is in the run. If the fish is actively feeding,

the movement will be consistent. If the trout is lethargic or resting, the movement will be sporadic.

When gazing into deep water, investigate every object in the run. You might see only a hint of red, which could be a trout with a gill plate the size of an apple. Other times, you might only see a hint of a different color. The point is to concentrate on subtle hints, not detailed objects. This is difficult because while you are looking in these dark, difficult areas, a sense of urgency can take over, making you feel rushed and discouraged. But focus on the water in front of you—slowly scan every inch for a good period of time.

In clear water, you would think finding the trout would be easy, but fish are masters at blending into their surroundings. From high vantage points, say looking down from the top of a trail or

Color Changes

Trout blend in with their surroundings, so it's best to look for water that will expose the fish and not give it cover. A brown trout the same color as a light tan cobblestone bottom would be exposed in areas of green vegetation.

Always look for the transitions of color in the river, whether it is a light-colored sandbar next to a deep run, or pieces of vegetation on a rocky bottom. Changes in color show different depths, expose structure, and are great areas for trout to hold and be noticed. These areas are critical to examine because they give you some of the most detailed images of the trout against contrasting colors.

Color changes help you spot fish. Trout will sometimes move out of one section of colored river bottom onto a sandbar, making them visible targets.

Even subtle color changes can be enough to show a trout's silhouette and give you a target to cast to.

rock formation, you might see a shadow or silhouette of a trout in a deep pool. From a lower vantage point, look for movement, most commonly from the fins, and for shadows cast on the river bottom or a vague silhouetted outline of the body if the fish is suspended.

Remember, if the fish are suspended, they are not as hard to see in the deep water. But if they are hugging low on the bottom, scanning the water for any movements or silhouettes is important.

Riffled Water

My favorite area to look for trout is in riffled runs. The constant disturbance in the water allows you to get close to the trout without being detected. Trout in these choppy waters usually have only a few seconds to react and eat the fly, and because of the speed with which they have to make a decision, they take the fly more readily than in slower water. Because the image is not clear, the take is often aggressive. These close encounters are great learning experiences because you can get close enough to see the trout and learn from its behavior.

The window

In these water conditions, the fish's image is distorted and hard to see. Look for movement, shadows, and dark silhouettes on the typically light river bottom. It is harder to see in flat water because you often can't get into a position that is ideal for seeing the trout and its movements. In riffled water, seeing is not easier but, because the trout's view is distorted, you can get into a better position. The first two things to look for are silhouettes of the trout and coloration or markings.

Rising fish in riffles are hard to see, especially if there is difficult glare. Each bump of the riffled water can look like a trout's head barely breaking the surface to sip in its meal. To determine if the bump is a head, look for a dark object on the surface or light reflecting off the trout's wet head.

Brown trout are great at disguising themselves because the color is on the bottom half of the fish. Like this beautiful specimen, the top half of the trout blends in with the river bottom, making it difficult to see in a riffled run.

You can also look for adult insects on the water and follow them downstream. Make sure you pick one adult and follow it through the course of the run. Or wait for an adult to land in the line or the seam of the water where you think the trout is feeding, and watch it float through the run. If you see it disappear, then you have a target.

When there is top water feeding activity, I look for a dark image against the water or the wake left after the trout has broken the surface. There is rarely a ring, like you would normally see in calm water, because the trout's mouth is acting as a rock would: forcing the water to split in two seams, one on either side of the object, leaving a wake on top.

These tips will help you locate more targets without relying on movement when your eyes are distracted by turbulent water. The tips work for slower moving water as well.

Sunglasses, binoculars, net, rod, and reel—choosing the proper tools is essential to a good day on the water.

CHAPTER 6

Tools for the Hunt

Considering the amount of gear available, choosing what is necessary is a challenge, especially when you become a collector or compulsive spender. I try to limit my gear to what is going to give me the upper hand—and nothing more. When fly fishers talk about gear, they generally mean rods, reels, lines, and waders—those sorts of things. For many anglers, items such as glasses, hats, and clothing are afterthoughts, yet for the sight-fishing angler, they are some of the most important tools. I always have certain tools with me—every time I look for trout.

Polarized Glasses

The most important tool in sight fishing for trout, or any species of fish for that matter, is a quality pair of polarized sunglasses. Without them, it is impossible to see trout under many light conditions because of glare. The better the quality, the better you can see.

Polarized lenses eliminate glare, which is light and bright colors reflecting or bouncing off the water's surface and into your eyes. Glare makes it difficult to see past the water's surface. Wherever there are horizontal surfaces producing glare, wearing polarizing lenses reduces eye fatigue.

A quality pair of sunglasses is essential in protecting the health of your eyes. The glasses block the UV rays and protect your eyes from problems such as glaucoma and cataracts. Good glasses reduce eyestrain and keep your eyes comfortable during a hard day of searching for trout in glare and bright conditions.

How do polarized lenses work? Peter Crow, president of Smith Optics, provided the following information: "The principal of polarization is the selective reduction of light rays. Light waves, traveling freely, can vibrate in any

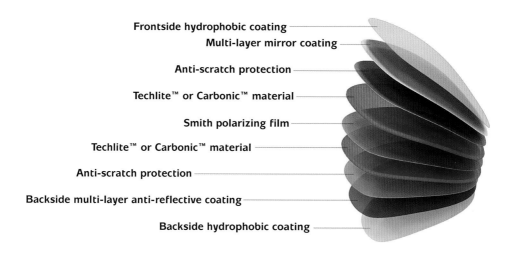

Frontside hydrophobic coating

Multi-layer mirror coating

Anti-scratch protection

Techlite™ or Carbonic™ material

Smith polarizing film

Techlite™ or Carbonic™ material

Anti-scratch protection

Backside multi-layer anti-reflective coating

Backside hydrophobic coating

Here is an example of the proper layering system to complete a polarized lens. SMITH OPTICS

direction, up and down, right to left, diagonally, etc. When light strikes a parallel-reflecting surface such as water or snow, it begins to vibrate horizontally, or left to right. A polarizing filter, usually sandwiched between two lenses, allows only the vertical light waves to enter, reducing glare. Polarized lenses tend to be expensive because of the lamination process required to join the lenses and polarizing filter together. The polarizing filters must be mounted so that their planes of polarization are aligned accurately or the effect is lost. Polarized lenses eliminate visually interfering glare. With cleaner light transmitting to the eye, colors become more vibrant and therefore somewhat intensified, due to the lack of glare."

Tint

When choosing the best tint, consider all the different lighting conditions you encounter when you are on the water. In bright conditions, a gray tint is ideal because it blocks out the intensely bright light. For low-light situations, a yellow or amber color is best to brighten the water in front of you. However, with the constant change in weather patterns in the course of one day or one week on any river in the world, it would be im-

Brown and copper are the best all-around lens tints for a wide range of conditions on the river.

possible to have either bright or low-light conditions that last all day. As a compromise, the best all-around tint is either copper or light brown. It is dark enough for bright days and light enough for dark days, and you won't have to change your glasses. This tint also intensifies red, greens, and blues, giving you better color visibility below the water's surface.

Peter Crow provided the following information about tint color: "Each lens tint has a specific transmission curve within the color spectrum. The gray-based lenses transmit light the most naturally. Conversely, a yellowish tint will cause some color shifting, but can provide more contrast, and more importantly, gather available light. This is a benefit in lower light conditions. The copper- and brown-based lenses provide a nice combination of relatively true color transmission and enhanced contrast. These are generally the lenses most favored by fly anglers."

There are interchangeable lenses that you can use with one frame; however, the challenge is that each lens tint will cause every image in the river to look different, making it difficult to develop a frame of reference. To overcome this obstacle, get familiar with how the trout will appear in the water when you change the lenses. Approach each lens color like you would if you were looking for trout in a new river. When you are looking through brown or copper lens, the reds, greens, and blues stand out more. If you change to an amber lens that lightens the water, colors are not as apparent. Instead, the silhouette of the trout will be more visible. Because you must learn how the trout will appear through each tint, practice using all the interchangeable lenses so that you are familiar with how the trout will appear with each lens. It is best to choose the lens based on the lighting conditions before you start fishing, and stick with that tint until there is a drastic change in lighting. That way there is less strain on your eyes from constantly changing lenses.

What I respect the most about clients is their determination to learn and be better each time they are on the water. George Torrison is one of many great anglers always ready for the hunt. ANGUS DRUMMOND

Photochromic lenses change tints depending on light levels. When UV rays are higher or when the sun is brighter, the lenses darken. When the UV rays are lower and the sunlight is dimmer, the lenses lighten. According to Peter Crow: "Photochromic is a feature enabling a lens to be UV sensitive, thereby lightening and darkening with various degrees of UV exposure. The brighter the condition (more UV), the darker the lens becomes.

This is a great pair of frames for sight fishing. Notice how the frame is thick around the sides, reducing side glare.

Conversely, the darker the condition (less UV), the lighter the lens becomes." I own a pair of these lenses and prefer them in situations when the lighting and UV rays are strong.

Finding the right frame

Reducing under- and side glare is a big challenge for a quality frame. Frames with thick sides that mold to your face and have large lenses that cover a wide area around your eyes will make you feel like you are looking out of a dark room.

While I prefer Smith Optics, with models such as the Hide Out, Shelter, and Fishbone, Oakley's Monster Dogs and Costa Del Mar's Black Fin do the job as well. These companies all provide high-end polarized sunglasses. Just make sure you get

the wraparound models—the frame should extend from your nose all the way around to the side of your face to eliminate side glare.

Once you find the right tint and the model that correctly fits your face, you have to choose glass or polycarbonate lenses. Polycarbonate lenses are cheaper, lighter, and have good impact resistance. However, glass has better scratch resistance and has the best polarized film, providing the clearest view. According to Peter Crow: "Glass is the lens material with the highest optical quality and has been a preference of trout anglers worldwide. Due to its hardness, it is the most scratch-resistant material available. The rigidity of glass makes it an excellent polarizing film host. Glass can be a heavier product and feel more substantial, but weight is not often a concern when a frame is well designed and fits the wearer properly. . . . Polycarbonate is a commonly used material in today's polarized sunglasses. The primary benefits of polycarbonate are impact resistance, weight, and price. Polycarbonate is the same material used in safety glasses and is impact resistant and the recommended lens for action sports. It is lighter in weight and a less expensive lens than glass."

In addition, certain manufacturers offer prescription polarized sunglasses in some models. If you cannot get a prescription in a specific model, there are companies that offer fit-over polarized glasses to wear over your prescription glasses.

As a full-time guide, I always prepare for every trip with a backup of every piece of equipment—just in case. The item that I most often give clients is a good pair of glasses. After using a quality pair of glasses, they learn what a difference it can make. Quality glasses are one of the most important selections of gear you can make, ranking right up there with your rod and reel. If you can see better, you will spot more targets and get a clear view of the river bottom, the trout, and its movements. Quality glasses are worth the investment.

The Buff

During the last few years of sight fishing, I have tried many ways to eliminate reflections from the water's surface that inhibit my vision. One useful tool I discovered is the Buff, a lightweight, highly

The Buff is the best deterrent for under-eye glare. The dark color under your eyes reduces glare dramatically, giving you a clearer view of the trout.

This angler is wearing a hat with a long bill to help reduce glare. A dark-colored under-brim prevents light from reflecting into his eyes.

breathable fabric that you wear around your face below your sunglasses, covering everything from your neck to your nose. Thanks to a gift from a client who was an avid saltwater fly angler, I realized that covering the bottom half of my face with dark material helps eliminate glare from the difficult sun that we have 300 days a year in Colorado. You can use a fleece balaclava, but they are prone to fogging your glasses when it is cold, and they are too warm in the summer. The Buff is breathable and comfortable enough to wear in warm weather.

Like a football player wearing black strips below his eyes to reduce glare from lights and camera flashes in a stadium, the Buff reduces any under-eye glare, especially in bright conditions, and shades your face to help you spot fish better. You can pull the material up to cover your nose, the side of your face, and your ears by placing it at an angle on the back of a ball cap. It will keep your skin protected and covered during the course of the day, preventing sunburn and protecting you from UV rays that can cause serious medical issues such as skin cancer. You may not have to use sunscreen on your face either, so you won't get sunscreen in your eyes.

Picking a Good Hat

The make and under-brim color of your hat can reduce glare and give you needed shade. There are many different makes, from the traditional cowboy hat to a newly designed wide-brim baseball cap. These top pieces complete the shadowed face-mask you want: you are trying to reduce glare from every angle and make your face a dark, non-reflecting shadow. The hat will make sure no light is reflected back to your eyes. Many anglers prefer the shade and sun protection of a Tilley or cowboy hat. Be sure the wide brim does not interfere with your peripheral vision.

Make sure whatever style you prefer has a dark color on the under-brim of the hat. This will keep the glare from bouncing off your brim back into your eyes. I prefer either a long brim or wide brim hat that casts a long shadow on my face, or acts like shadowed side shields. Pick a subtle color that will blend in with the surroundings on the river you are fishing. This will keep the trout from noticing the tallest part of your body. Wide brim or Tilley hats supply shade around your head, but I do not like them because the wide brim obscures my peripheral vision, preventing me from detecting movement.

Binoculars

I learned about this overlooked tool from watching Doug Swisher's videos in the mid-1980s. Swisher used a pair of quality binoculars to determine exactly how the trout were rising and what particular insect was attracting them. How many times have you seen a rise and tied on a dry based on what you saw flying overhead or floating at your feet in the slowest current of the water? That flying or floating fly may not be what the fish is feeding on midstream.

In a complex hatch of multiple insects, trout will not always make the same riseform every time. Different insects may result in multiple riseforms. For instance, during the early part of July with numerous adult insects hatching at the same time, I saw a huge Trico cloud and some mixed species of mayflies flying about. Sure enough, after trial and error, I found the trout keying in on Pale Morning Duns before the Tricos fell to the water's surface.

With binoculars you can see what insect is on the water's surface, and you can watch the fish's riseforms. Binoculars can make the difference between good dry-fly action and a tough day on the water.

When you are select a pair of binoculars, look for the best quality in the smallest model. Choose the highest power possible in your price range, ultimately allowing you to view a trout up close from thirty or more feet away. I have a pair that fits in my jacket pocket or my fanny pack. I always have them on me, in a Ziploc bag, ready to use when I need them. Binoculars take the guessing game out of many top-water situations when visibility with the naked eye is challenging.

Many of your most effective casts will be within 10 feet of the trout—as long as you can wade that close. When I talk about the nuances of sight fishing, I always emphasize the short game. JAY NICHOLS

CHAPTER 7

The Approach

With the right approach and planning, you can get extremely close to a trout before making a cast. Your casts are much more precise and drifts are better when you are close to the fish; trying to bomb out 20 or 30 feet of fly line and make complicated mends to combat the currents is difficult. Your most effective casts will be when you are within 10 feet of the trout—as long as you can wade that close. When I talk about the nuances of sight fishing, I emphasize the short game.

This chapter is full of tips on how to approach trout. The techniques may seem simple. However, you can easily forget them when you spot a large fish, get excited, and rush the situation. Take time to analyze your surroundings and the water before you start to fish, and determine the best plan of attack before you move into position.

You must be prepared and ready to cast when you spot a fish. Fumbling with your line or tackle wastes precious time and decreases your chances of success. Speed is important: you can get more drifts to the fish, see more trout in a run, and not waste precious time casting to a spooky fish. Most trout in shallow water are wary, and you may only get a few good shots before the fish spooks or stops feeding. Most trout you encounter when you are sight fishing are more aware of their surroundings than a fish you cannot see. To keep you on your toes, imagine that you are a trout below the water's surface, and every shadow, movement, or glint of light coming from above could be a threat or predator wanting you for a meal.

If you have more than one way to present the fly to a fish, you have a huge advantage when you are dealing with different water currents, structure, and riverside obstacles—whether you are fishing dry flies, nymphs, or streamers. I wish every approach were the same at a specific angle, but this is never the

You have only a few moments to make a presentation to the fish before it detects you. That's why you have to be ready to cast accurately. After a long day at the ready, Brandon Lenderink is rewarded with this late evening brown.

case. Even if you are in the ideal spot when you first approach, you may have to adjust and move farther upstream or downstream. You may need to do this to get a proper drift, or because of uneven currents or the unusual position the trout is holding in the water. Sometimes you'll be in position to make a great cast, but then the fish will move or drift a few feet away from where it was. To be successful, you have to adjust quickly.

One of a trout's favorite places to hold is around rocks or boulders. Trout love these areas for the cover and complex currents, but the rocks present a challenge to the angler. One of my favorite spots to target trout is in the cushion in front of boulders where the river bottom is washed out, which creates a pocket where trout hold. In this situation, get across or slightly downstream of the trout and use the structure as cover. If the trout drifts to either side of the rock, which it will often do, compensate by pulling the line in and moving downstream a

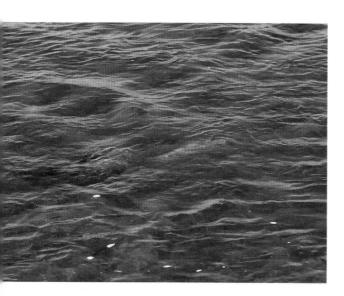

Trout holding in front of rocks present challenges. The best approach is from the side; a side approach allows you to get into position without spooking the trout.

When you cast from above the trout always keep a low profile to avoid spooking the fish.

few feet. If the fish moves to the far seam, avoid casting through the fast seam breaking around the rock by moving upstream to get a drift while your line remains above the faster current.

These quick and constant adjustments to your approach are critical. Trout do not stay still when they are feeding hard, so you need to adjust to their movement. Also, when trout spook, not all of them will bolt up- or downstream, disappearing in the river. In fact, many trout will simply swim a few feet and start feeding again, and you have to go after them.

Here are three ways to get your cast off quicker: the speed cast, rigged and ready, and the angle. Do not limit these ready positions to only one particular approach. As you will see, you can use them from different angles.

Upstream of the Fish

I like to sight-fish upstream of the trout. This is an effective yet challenging way to present your flies to the fish because you are in the trout's viewing lane. It is a great way to achieve what I call the dead swing. Being able to get a tension drift or drag-free drift with a swing at the end increases your chances of fooling more trout—with two presentations wrapped into one. During a hatch when the adults are dancing or drifting on the water's surface, you can cover a run with a drag-free or tension drift at the first half of the drift, and then allow your flies to swing toward the edge of the river like a skittering, diving, or drowned adult. This will let you give the trout the presentation they want—with or without movement.

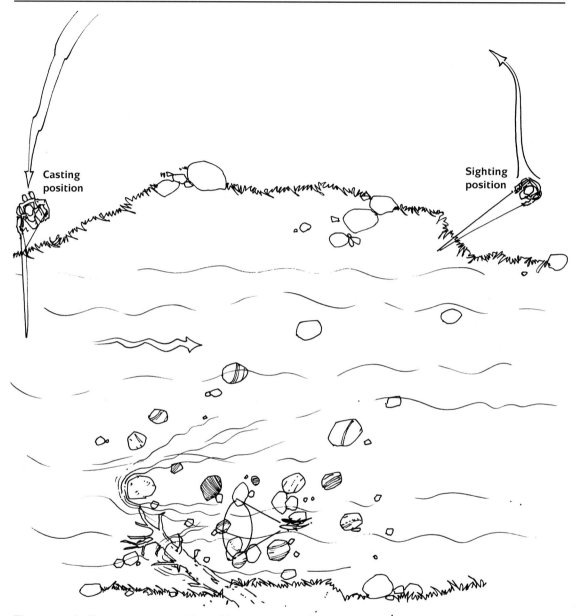

Casting
position

Sighting
position

The approach: If you spot a trout while walking upstream, and you want to cast to it from above, walk wide of the fish, staying out of the trout's field of view. Stay low as you move into position, and remain low as you cast.

When caddis are popping in late May and the trout are exploding on the surface and willing to move to slam the fly, swinging flies downstream is awesome. That is a good time to "make like a rock" and wait for the trout to rest before it takes another fly. When it does, set the hook, lift the rod smoothly, keeping the rod slightly horizontal to cushion the tippet. This technique is just as effective in subsurface conditions when trout are looking for emerging adults, or when the trout

The Speed Cast

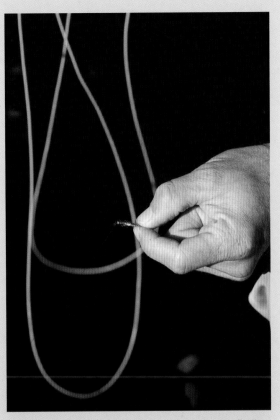

1. To be in the ready position for a fast presentation to the trout, first figure out how much excess line you will need. Place that amount of line under your index finger and your ring finger.

2. Once you have gained control of the excess fly line, place the fly in between the thumb and index finger of your non-casting hand. For a proper release without snagging your finger, pinch the fly at the bend of the hook.

(continued on next page)

sees a meal that is moving toward the surface. It can consume the meal without having to expose itself to a predator from above.

This presentation works best in shallow water where the trout's viewing lane is small and narrow, or if the water is off-colored. Remember to first spot the fish from an approach *downstream*. Once you spot the fish, study it for a while to figure out its activities and feeding be-

havior so that you know how to properly present your flies.

Before you creep into position upstream of the fish, find something to use as a marker—a rock in the river or a willow on the river's edge—so that you have a reference point when you move. You might be able to see the fish when you are downstream of it, but your viewing lane or window will be completely different when you move upstream,

3. Before casting, release the fly line under your ring finger, allowing the extra line to fall to the water. This makes it easier for the line to shoot through the guides when you cast, preventing tangles.

4. When you begin the back cast, keep the fly line, leader, and flies airborne—in that sequence. This will prevent the fly or flies from ticking the water surface, causing a disturbance that could spook a wary trout.

and glare (or something else) might prevent you from seeing the fish easily. So having a marker is critical. If you are fishing with a partner, one of you can be the spotter and direct the casting angler to the trout (see chapter 15).

Once you have a marker, walk wide around the river to prevent spooking the fish back to the river's edge upstream. Because being upstream of the fish can put you in its line of sight, be ready to

cast quickly. Be careful not to make a lot of movement getting the fly to the fish.

When you are still downstream of the fish, pull out enough line to reach your target. This minimizes your motions when you are in the trout's field of view. Then pull back the line you have out, leaving two or three feet past the rod tip. With the remaining line, make two big loops and place them between your thumb and index finger while

5. Smoothly accelerate, then stop abruptly at 1 o'clock. For the back cast, the rod should be at an upward 45-degree angle behind you. This will allow the fly line to unroll up and above any structure there.

6. Once the rod tip has stopped and the fly line, leaders, and flies are straightened out behind you, begin the forward cast while keeping your wrist straight.

(continued on next page)

holding the rod handle. After you have your line in place, grab the last fly on your rig, and hold it between your index finger and thumb by the bend of the hook with the opposite hand. This is a common practice used in saltwater, but it is overlooked by trout anglers.

When you are in place upstream, drop the line between your fingers; make one roll cast forward releasing all the line in front of you; load the rod with one backcast; and present the fly on the forward cast with the rod tip ending just above the surface of the water. This is the best ready position from upstream because you eliminate any false casting or multiple rod movements that might spook the trout. After you stop your rod tip to deliver the flies, allow the leader to straighten out, making the flies the first thing to come into the trout's viewing lane. Stop the rod tip at nine o'clock;

7. To ensure maximum power in the cast, smoothly accelerate the rod forward by pushing the rod in a downward motion.

8. While the rod is traveling to the stopping point of 9 o'clock, allow the line to gradually shoot through the guides.

then gradually drop the rod to the water's surface. When you follow the flies downstream, keep your rod tip low so that you do not spook the fish.

Across-Stream from the Fish

This approach gives you the best view of the trout, and it is easier to cast accurately from this angle than if you are above or below the trout.

The key is to remain slightly downstream of the fish so you do not risk spooking it, and to wade carefully so the trout will not feel the vibration as you move through the water. It is surprising to most people how close you can get to the target without spooking it if you are careful.

The best position is on a low bank or at water level. This keeps you out of the trout's viewing lane, and your casting will go unnoticed. From this

9. When executed correctly, the rod is pointed in the direction of the cast, with the slack line straightened out above the trout.

when you are across from the fish, allowing your flies to pass through the trout's viewing lane but short enough to prevent lining the trout.

Shallow water

Shallow water—two to three feet deep—creates the biggest challenge. The fish's viewing lane is small and narrow and the sinking rate is fast, so your options for adjustment are limited. The key to success is to think short, having the flies drift two to six inches to the side of the trout, not directly to the fish, so that you don't snag, rub, or spook the target. When you are in shallow water, you don't have the luxury of casting farther upstream of the trout and then making adjustments: the flies will snag on the river bottom before they reach the fish. Setups presented slightly short of the trout, two to three feet above the fish, give the fish a chance to turn and take the fly.

Standard depth

In water depths of three or four feet, place the split shot in line above the trout, with the extension of your fly or flies past the drift to compensate for the natural drift back toward you. You can apply a small mend during the presentation: keep tension on the flies while they drift, but allow a small amount of slack to compensate for the sinking ratio. The advantage to keeping tension when you are drifting flies at this depth or shallower is that you prevent the trout from detecting unnatural objects such as split shot, leader, or strike indicators

Deep water

In deep water of five to eight feet, the challenge is that you can't adjust your presentation downstream. The key is to fool the trout into believing that your rig and presentation looks natural. While still using the dotted line as a direction when your flies are drifting downstream to the trout, make sure you cast far enough to allow your flies time to sink. Don't exaggerate your mends to keep

angle you must always stay as low and as close to the water's surface as possible. It can be as simple as hunching over to get close to the water's surface, or as extreme as lying on your belly or side. As long as you stay low and never try to walk upstream of the trout—even one step—you will be more successful. This is a prime area to get a drift and to view the trout, but it can be risky if you cast too far across-stream. So always think short

Bill "Beatle" Abshagen was able to land this hefty male rainbow in low, clear water by watching its feeding behavior. The water was so clear when I was spotting for him on the high bank that I had to lay on my belly to stay out of sight of the trout. The hardest part was to not rush the situation, and to wait for the male 'bow to close its mouth before I hollered, "Lift!"

your line taut. The main thing when dealing with deep-water sight-fishing situations at a short distance is to start with a light weight on your rig, and then gradually work your way down by adding more weight or weighted flies.

All deep-water rigs can be used with or without a strike indicator. If you use a strike indicator, adjust by trial and error until you achieve the cor-

Always start your across-stream approach slightly downstream of the trout. Once you are in position, slowly inch your way upstream until you are across from the fish. ROSS PURNELL

Watch Your Rod Tip

Sight fishing is a game of close encounters. Even the simplest steps such as rod positioning mean the difference between landing the trout and never seeing it again. Many anglers don't realize that the rod tip can spook trout. I always keep the rod tip low at water level whether looking for trout, changing flies, or getting ready to cast. Too many times I have seen a trout that was happily feeding spooked by a rod tip wagging around in the air.

You should also keep your rod tip low when you are drifting your flies to a trout in shallow or clear water. While high-stick fishing works in many deep-water situations, a high rod can spook fish in clear water. If you keep the rod tip low, and follow your flies as they drift downstream, you can keep tension with your presentation, allowing you to adjust as needed. You have a tighter line, which makes for better hook sets, and the low rod pre-vents your flies from being pulled toward you (and away from the trout's path) as they drift.

Unfortunately, you cannot always cast with the rod low. When you are casting dry flies perpendicular to the trout, false-cast downstream of the fish to keep any moving objects out of the trout's view. And sometimes you need to follow the fish with your rod tip high to prevent snagging the river's edge or bottom and to keep your flies clean. For example, if I spot a trout that is upstream, I slowly move along the river's edge to get into position; then I'll keep my rod high to prevent snagging vegetation, grass, willows, and structure. Strip in some fly line while keeping your rod tip at a 45-degree position downstream; be sure to keep it out of the trout's view. This cast will skate your flies on the water's surface, preventing you from catching anything before you reach your final destination.

Rigged for traveling. Place the fly on the second or third guide, and wrap the remaining leader around the back of the reel. Then when you are going to cast, take the leader from around the reel and tap the rod above the guide where the flies are rigged. This will drop the fly off the guide so you can quickly cast to the trout. See **Rigged and ready** on page 80.

When you approach from downstream, keep a close eye on the trout because the glare will change on the water's surface when you adjust to this low position. First I locate the trout from across-stream; then I approach from below and cast where I spotted the fish.

rect depth to suspend the flies so they drift the length of the run. If you choose to not use a strike indicator, you can achieve maximum drift without snagging by applying tension to the flies and lifting the rod tip. This is similar to high-stick nymphing—the rod travels in line with the flies and leader as they drift downstream. Alternatively, and similar to Czech nymphing, you can lead the flies and the leader with the rod tip, creating tension through the leader and rig.

Rigged and ready

Most fly rods have hook keepers, small metal loops just above the cork handle designed to hold your bottom fly when you are not fishing. If you see a fish and your fly is hooked on the hook keeper, it takes time to strip out enough fly line so that you can cast. To save a little extra time and commotion, you can gain up to three feet by hooking the fly (or the last fly in the multiple-fly rig) to the second or third guide of your rod above the cork handle and wrapping the line around the backside of the reel foot. If your leader is 9-feet long, this will leave a few feet of fly line already outside of the tip, so you can deliver your fly more efficiently.

Downstream from the Trout

The safest way to approach a trout holding in a river is from downstream so that you are in its blind spot. You are invisible to the fish if you wade cautiously and do not cast over the fish. This is the best approach when casting dry flies because the only thing that lands above the fish is your leader,

tippet, and flies, and in water with an even current speed, the flies will drift back toward you, drag-free. As long as your flies land softly, the fish will not spook.

If the currents are tricky, or if you are you are imitating subsurface food, get into position at a 45-degree angle below the trout. This allows you to present the flies to the trout while keeping the fly line, indicator, or weight out of the trout's viewing lane. If you cast directly below the trout using subsurface imitations, the trout may detect split shot, indicator, or fly line, and it won't take your flies. This is why the 45-degree angle down-

When you are walking upstream, save time by having the correct amount of line already out of your rod tip so that you can quickly cast to the fish without a lot of false casting.

Brown trout like this quality male love bad weather because they have more cover from dark skies and disturbances on the water's surface. But in these conditions, it is difficult to see them, so your presentation and approach are crucial.

side of the trout from a low tuck position, and then present the fly after the final backcast. The line won't hover above the trout and spook it. This is incredibly effective when you are fishing calm water where any disturbance on the water's surface can put the fish down.

This approach works in many situations: when trout are moving and you need to make a presentation every time the trout stops at a new location; or if you have spooked the fish but you can still see it and you want to move into position to cast again after the fish has settled and begins to feed once more. It allows you to make a fast presentation when you are sighting and approaching water where you know there are trout, and you need to make a quick presentation. Many times I have spotted a fish early in the day, made a presentation,

stream of the fish is so important when you are presenting anything other than dry flies. When nymphing, you are better off perpendicular or upstream of the trout because you can see better and you can control your drift better.

Tip tension

Make sure your rod tip or fly line is not pointed up at the target until you present the fly. You do this by keeping five to ten feet of fly line past the rod tip drifting on the water behind as you approach the trout. Then, when you need to determine the distance to reach the fish, cast to either

In tough lighting conditions, a good way to spot a fish is from a high bank. However, the higher you are, the easier it is for fish to detect you. So approach with caution and always work upstream. Note that this angler has two rods rigged, so he is ready for any encounter.

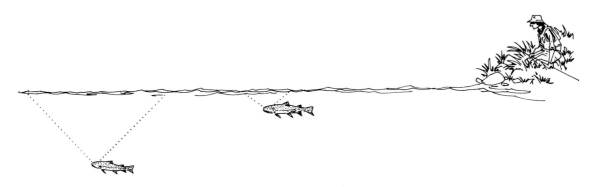

Trout's cone of vision. The deeper the trout holds, the wider his viewing lane is.

and the fish spooked. Later that same day, knowing that my target could be nervous and would spook if there was any movement from above, I made one last cast: my only opportunity to present the fly to the fish.

The true advantage to this ready position is that you can pull line out or strip line in before you cast. This eliminates false casting. You can move about a run or section of water quickly while still remaining stealthy and accurate with every cast. I use one version of this cast in the wind. On the South Platte River in South Park, a giant, wind-swept valley, casting in 20 to 30 mph winds is frustrating. To avoid huge knots and tangles, position yourself with the wind in your face, then simply lift your rod to a twelve o'clock position and hold it there. The wind will straighten your line, leader, and flies behind you. This technique keeps the rod loaded and ready for a forward cast.

Bank Approaches

From a high vantage point, you can see all of the action of a trout stream unfolding below you. Trout holding deep in dark or turbulent water are comfortable and usually not wary of predators from above because they do not see any movement. Casting to these fish from the high bank is fine—as long as you are able to react and drop

quickly once you spot the fish. Take the time to consider which bank is best for the approach. I love to cast to a fish from a high bank where I can see the trout's every movement.

When casting from a high position, any movement will increase the chance of spooking the trout. So adjust the line or distance of the cast high above the fish to reach the right depth. The trout will stay in the lane if it feels secure, and you will get more quality presentations. If the fish are spooky and are in shallow water, stay low.

In shallow water, or when trout are hugging the bank, you find yourself in unusual casting positions—even lying on your belly, if that's what it takes. It is harder to see the fish when you are close to the water's surface, but it is equally difficult for the trout to spot you.

My closest encounters with trout, especially big ones, are from low banks. I prefer to spot the trout from a high position and then move across the river downstream and creep into position on the low bank. The trout only detects the line, leader, or flies if the cast is off or if there is too much false casting. If you can eliminate movement and use the casting techniques you learn in this book, you will have more undetected drifts. If you approach each of these encounters understanding that one bad cast will spook fish, you will automatically become more cautious, and more effective, in your approaches.

Dressing for the Hunt

Like gear, apparel is a tool. On my home waters in Colorado, I fish in places with open sky where I wear a subtle blue jacket and brown or tan waders. The lower half of my body resembles foliage on the river's edge, and my upper torso resembles a familiar color of the blue sky.

When you select your apparel—from waders to hat—look for subtle colors that match your surroundings. You'll have a better chance to sneak up on a trout when you don't contrast with the natural colors. I prefer tans, greens, and browns in natural shades. Anglers on the East Coast, where the vegetation is lush and green, are better served with darker colors to blend in with their background.

For extremely wary fish, you may need to go with camouflaged clothing. I personally have not had many situations where I felt that I needed to wear camouflage, but I would in a split second, if that's what it took. Remember that trout are looking up when they see you, so you want to blend in with not just the surroundings on the river's edge, but also with what is above you. This is why you commonly see New Zealand guides in camouflage, because they are perched in a tree on the river's edge, giving instructions to their clients.

A bright watch or metal forceps can be a problem. This is why forceps, watches, and nippers are now available in dark colors that won't reflect light. Remember: while you are hunting a target, the target might be looking at you.

Always try to imagine how much the trout can see and how big its viewing lane is. Imagine a viewing lane shaped like an ice cream cone on top of the trout's head. The deeper the water, the wider the viewing lane. The shallower the water, the narrower the lane. In deep water, the trout's viewing lane is wider because the cone above the trout's head is larger.

Take your time covering the water, and if you can, approach with the sun at your back. I always scan a good twenty feet or more ahead. That gives me time to get low before approaching the trout, and I can determine if what I am looking at is a trout. If you are scanning only a few feet ahead, the trout will see you and will spook before you have the chance to see it.

This angler's apparel matches his surroundings so that he can get close enough to the fish to spot them.

High banks are great for spotting fish, but they are not good to fish from. Not only do you run the risk of spooking more fish, but it is difficult to follow your presentation from a high bank while keeping your rod low. This means that you often have to move into the best position after you have spotted the fish. Low bank sides are not as ideal for spotting fish, but you are in a better position to present the fly.

Body Posture

When approaching trout, stay low to the ground and out of view. If you are casting from land, do so on one knee; if you are wading, hunch over. (Remember, the deeper you wade, the more you reduce your height.) Taking a knee allows you to push off with the knee that is not on the ground, which gives you better balance and allows you to move more quickly. If you are casting to a trout on both knees, your legs get tired and it is difficult to keep your balance when you stand up.

Another trick I use is what I call the toe dive. I noticed that when many anglers wade a river they shuffle their feet, even in shallow water. I'm sure this is because it's how people are taught to wade, and it's easier because your feet are always close to the river bottom. Now, I know this is a safe way to wade, and yes, I do the same in fast water when I do not want to take a drink. However, when I am moving upriver stalking a trout and I want to prevent vibrations or noise in the water, I will pick one foot up as high as I can and then point my toe down for each step I take. The foot is diving into the water, causing less disturbance. In many tough situations, this technique has helped me get extremely close to the fish.

Trout are not the only salmonid that take a careful, low, bank side approach. These brightly-colored arctic char/ Dolly Varden were very spooky. After a few days of hunting, Shannon Korpi was able sneak up on this fresh buck.

To prevent the fish from detecting you, hide behind structure when you are casting to wary trout, especially in calm water.

CHAPTER 8

Tippin' and Sippin': Reading Rises

Over the years, I have tried to learn something new on the water every day. I figure that knowing is better than guessing. Take the time to watch the trout while it is feeding on the surface; that observation will help you determine how best to present your fly to the fish. Rising trout move in many different ways because they adapt to the water they are in and the movements of the bugs (or other food items).

Once you understand basic riseforms, the most critical aspect of sight fishing with dry flies is making every cast count. Economy of motion—not wasting any time—are important to your strategy, affecting everything from fly selection to approach presentation. We have been taught—through movies like *A River Runs Through It,* pictures, casting competitions—that to be successful in dry-fly fishing we must be able to false cast tight loops at a great distance. But to cast to the best of your ability, you need to eliminate all unnecessary motions in order to get your presentations to the trout. When I cast to a pod of fifteen trout that are sipping Tricos on the water's surface so aggressively that the surface is boiling, I make one false cast (or in many situations one backcast), to reload my rod, minimize movement, and wick moisture away; and then I make the presentation to the trout. That makes me more precise, with a pickup and lay-down presentation, and I don't have to reposition my fly on the water's surface after false casting. And I don't spook the fish: there is no line moving over the trout's head or spraying the water with drips. By keeping my fly in the water more, I get more presentations and more hookups.

To cast to a pod of rising trout, start at the back of the pod and select one fish to cast to. Then work upstream and pick off one trout at a time without spooking the rest of the pod. ANGUS DRUMMOND

Tippin' and Sippin'

When trout consume flies floating on the surface of calm water, they tip their heads upward by rotating their pectoral fins. They lift their heads to the water's surface to sip in a dry, leaving a dimple on the surface of the water. This is the most common riseform that I see. The trout does not expose a lot of its body every time it consumes a meal, preventing it from becoming much of a target to predators above. Since the fish does not have to expend unnecessary energy to eat, it is easier to consume multiple insects in the course of a hatch. Trout in rivers can be lazy. Unlike a trout residing in a large body of water such as a

There is nothing like watching the red stripe of a large rainbow suspended just below the water's surface. Every minute or so, the giant gill plate is exposed as it sips in a meal, making the trip complete for Timm Tews.

When you see a trout that is slowly tipping and sipping in clear water, wait until the trout has taken the fly before you set the hook. Here, a 15-pound 'bow is sipping midges on the surface.

reservoir, where it has to be in constant motion in search of food, the river's current brings the insect to the fish, so it does not have to expend as much energy to feed.

When trout are sipping in adults, remember that in some waters a smaller ring means you are dealing with a larger trout. But I have also witnessed trout in excess of 15 pounds rise to sip in a meal and have a quarter of its body break the water's surface. It may be that such a large body mass rising in the water column requires more energy, and each rise becomes more exhausting. This is why you may see more of a large trout's body out of the water. It is called a head rise because you see the entire head of the trout above the water's surface.

If you encounter trout feeding in large pods, start at the back of the pack. Observe the rest of the trout to determine the best location to cast from to keep from spooking the whole pod. Make sure that all of your casts are downstream of the pod to prevent them from detecting your movement. After you hook a trout in the back of the pod, try to gain control of the fight as soon as possible to prevent the fish from running upstream and spooking the others.

Selecting one trout, primarily the independent feeder, ensures that you are dealing with a larger trout. You can usually determine this by the size of the trout's head as it breaks the surface, or the large ring it leaves when it takes an insect. More of the body of a smaller trout is exposed when it feeds. Large fish are usually dominant in the water where they hold and feed. They naturally feed in areas with greater quantities of the food and at the head of the pod, where the largest trout has the first opportunity to consume a meal.

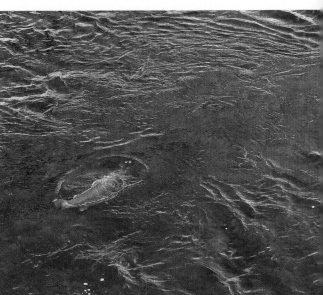

This chrome rainbow came up aggressively to eat a caddis, and it was as if someone had thrown a bowling ball into the water. My client and I jumped back because we were so startled.

Trout make this riseform when feeding on emergers, midges, mayflies, and terrestrials. I have even seen this riseform when fish were feeding on rodents such as mice. It is extremely important to see just what the trout is sipping off the water's surface before you start to fish.

The Splash

When a trout aggressively feeds on adults moving on the water's surface, especially caddis, it often powers up out of the water, consumes its food, and then goes back down, splashing the water with its tail. While this is the easiest riseform to detect, that fish can be a challenge to catch. When a trout comes to the surface with that much force, it risks missing its meal. So to prevent a break off, you must be patient and wait for the trout to go underwater before you set the hook. If you set early, you might be setting while the trout is moving upward: if you are pulling back with equal power, the tippet may reach its breaking point. This tests the nerves of even the most experienced dry-fly anglers. The nice thing about splashy rises is that you can see them in both calm and turbulent water. It's best to wait until the trout has finished the aggressive feeding behavior, and then set. Because the fish is concentrating so hard on catching the food source, the power of the rise will keep it from detecting that the fly is unnatural. You have an extra second for the fish's head to submerge, knowing the trout will not reject or spit the imitation while you wait.

The Drift

Vince Marinaro's observations from his book *A Modern Dry Fly Code* (1950) describe the compound rise as an extension of the simple rise. The trout drifts downstream while investigating the adult or imitation on the surface and decides whether to take or refuse the meal. This is a common rise, when trout have time to investigate their food source and are less confident. I like to call this rise "the drift." When I explain it to my clients, I tell them the trout is drifting downstream to investigate the fly but may also be hesitant to break the water's surface for fear of predators from above. The drift is not always aggressive. Most of the time trout choose the drift while they are preparing to eat the food source, and they drift slightly downstream as they lose the control to hold in the current.

I will never forget one experience on the Green River in Utah. Brown trout drifted downstream 15 to 20 feet, nudging the dry with their noses one or two times before they ate. This drove me and my partners nuts; I cannot tell you how many times I would set as the trout bumped my fly. I believe they acted this way to make sure it was not going to escape and to make sure it was a meal. A drag-free drift was vital.

Whenever I think of drifting trout feeding on the surface I remember a trip to the Green River with my good friends Eric Mondragon and Carl Emerson. The Green is notorious for selective trout on top water, especially during the famous cicada hatch. The fish there rattle the nerves of any experienced angler.

Before our venture to the Green, we heard stories of how difficult it was to time the cicada hatch and how exciting the fishing could be if you got it just right. With careful planning, we headed

up to the river in June when the river is usually swarming with cicadas. We arrived at Flaming Gorge Lodge, and to our surprise, we were met with high flows exceeding 4000 cubic feet per second. After our first afternoon of fishing with minimal success, I turned to Eric and said, "You can't win them all." We all had a good attitude and hoped that the next day our luck would change.

The next day, after meeting our guides in the morning and discussing our day's plans over a cup of coffee and breakfast, the stars aligned. Cicadas were in full force, and high waters created large eddies for aggressively rising trout. This sparked the beginning of a two-day top-water trip that my friends and I will never forget.

Before launching the drift boat on our first day, the guides told us to be patient in setting the hook

In this photograph you can see the result of a compound riseform. The trout followed and investigated the dry. Then it committed and its body angled to a straight vertical position as it sipped in the fly. ANGUS DRUMMOND

Here is a drifting Green River brown. You have to be rock steady until you are sure the trout has taken your fly, and then set. ANGUS DRUMMOND

when the fish came up to eat our cicada imitations. For most anglers, hesitating on the hook set or waiting for a trout to take a dry off the surface means a one-second delay. Well, after missing four or five fish, we soon learned that this waiting game could last up to five seconds. With cicadas buzzing around and falling to the surface like meteorites, we thought the excitement could not get any better. But after watching browns race to the surface half an inch below my fly, and bump it with their noses three or four times before sucking it in, my eyes were wide open and my hands were shaking. It was the most astounding feeding behavior I have ever seen from a trout drifting downstream. As we shared a few drinks at the end of the first day, Eric, Carl, and I were laughing at how many fish we missed because we thought the bumps on our fly were actual takes. Instead, the fish were playing tricks on us.

The U-Turn

If a trout turns downstream from its normal upstream feeding position, most of the time it will speed up to consume the dry fly, and then turn back to its original feeding location. From an angler's view, after the trout has consumed the dry and then gets back into its original position, it looks like a U-turn, similar to what you do when you are driving down the road with bad directions and you need to get back on track. Marinaro called this a complex rise. It is common in calm water where the fish gets a chance to inspect an insect slowly drifting downstream, or when slow water meets fast water, speeding up the downstream drift of the food.

Head-to-Tail and Headless

Trout make a head-to-tail rise, also called a porpoise or rolling rise, when they are feeding on dead or small insects on the surface film of the water. When the trout does commit to take a natural, it is typically so close to the water's surface that you can see the head, tail, and dorsal fin break the water's surface every time it eats. When you see this rise, investigate where the food source is. Sometimes the trout is eating adults on the surface; other times the fish is eating in or just below

Once a dry fly has moved past the trout's viewing lane, the fish will turn and follow it downstream, if it is not willing to allow the food to escape.

When the trout has turned downstream to consume the escaping meal, it speeds up to get ahead of the insect.

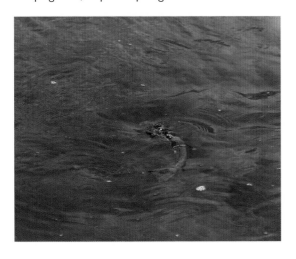

the film. If you see backs and tails on the rise but you cannot see the head breaking the surface—the headless head-to-tail rise—the fish is not taking adults on the surface or the film.

The Pounce

The pounce is the ultimate riseform. The trout rises, often from deep water or under some sort of structure, leaps out of the water with its body fully exposed, and then pounces down on the dry with its mouth wide open. This is a common riseform in Alaska, where anglers skate hoppers, mice, or brightly colored dry flies. I believe the trout are trying to ensure they will be able to consume their food source—or drown it, and have a second chance of attack when both the meal and the fish are submerged, even at the expense of using so much energy. While this is a rare riseform, it does occur, and it takes a lot of patience on your end to not set the hook too quickly.

The Gulp

When trout are eagerly eating lots of spent or dead insects, such as during a Trico hatch, there may be a film of food covering the water's surface. The trout will thrust its tail while opening its mouth and gulping in many insects at one time before going underwater. With so much vacuum-like suction coming from the mouth of a large trout, listen for a gulp or popping sound that can be heard from a fair distance away.

I have seen fish stay on the surface for up to three seconds with their mouths open—as if they are vacuuming the surface, engulfing as many insects as possible. When this occurs, the trout gets

The trout gains ground on the food source, and then rushes to be downstream of it. The rise resembles a U-turn, as the trout lifts up and turns to take the insect off the surface. ANGUS DRUMMOND

A brown trout is rising to drowned Tricos just below the water's surface. Investigate the riseform by watching the trout to determine if it is actually breaking the surface or feeding just below the surface.

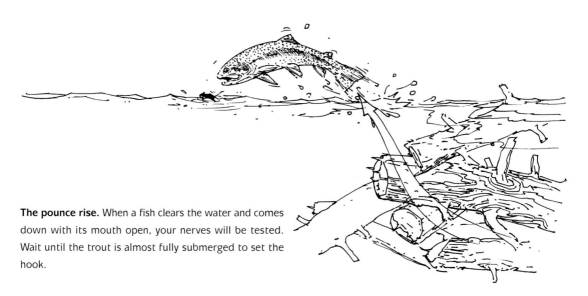

The pounce rise. When a fish clears the water and comes down with its mouth open, your nerves will be tested. Wait until the trout is almost fully submerged to set the hook.

into a feeding rhythm. There are two key things to remember about gulping or vacuuming trout on the water's surface: First, timing is critical for success. For example, if a fish comes up to eat and takes a one-second break, prepare your presentation so that your fly lands before the feeding pattern begins again. I tell my clients to wait for the trout to yawn and then stick it in its mouth. Second, while

these fish are so active and out of the water for long periods, they are vulnerable and aware of any subtle movement, whether it's vibration from wading in the water or a fly line casting overhead. So be sure to have your stopwatch and nerves of steel the next time you encounter gulping trout.

In calm water, the challenge is to determine if the trout is breaking the surface when it feeds, or

This brown is getting ready to eat a mouse. The mouse was floating dead on the surface and we waited downstream to see if a trout would take advantage of it. This fish should be good for a while after a meal like that. ANGUS DRUMMOND

if it is only brushing the surface with its back when it takes an emerger below the water film. Watch the tip of the trout's jaw break the surface, or the explosion of water and fish after an escaping adult has fallen victim. If this does not work, a bubble with a ring left on the surface is a dead giveaway that the fish is eating top water. This happens when the trout closes its mouth below the surface after eating an adult insect on the surface, and a bubble of air is pushed through the trout's gills.

Reacting to Trout Behavior

One of the best ways to fish dry flies is to watch their feeding behavior, the behavior of their prey, and the movement of the water in which they are rising. Riseforms are not the same for every in-sect. You can watch a trout perform five different riseform dances in sequence, one after another, to insects drifting downstream.

Sometimes, the largest trout in a pod, like this rainbow, may leave only the slightest disturbance on the water's surface. The only way to detect this trophy was by the bubble it left after consuming an adult.

The rise of a trout when it clears the water and pounces on the mouse to drown it and consume its meal is the ultimate top-water take.

Behavior based on insect activity

When you watch insects on the water and pay attention to how the trout eat them, you may be surprised. Based on what you read, you may think that trout rise a certain way for certain insects. But after logging hours on the water, I noticed trout aggressively splashing the surface to take a spinner drifting downstream, trout tipping and sipping to consume a hopper blown off the river's edge, and head-to-tail rises while trout were consuming caddis in the late evening. At first this was a surprise, but then I started to understand that the trout were simply responding to the insect's behavior. The same insect behaves in different ways, depending on the conditions. I realized that the best way to sight-fish dry flies is to match the behavior more than the hatch.

To adjust how you present the fly, take a step back and watch an adult drifting downstream. Watch the reaction from the trout when it takes the food source. If the fly is moving or fluttering on the surface when the fish take, you know that movement to your fly will result in more takes. If the fish are feeding with sipping rises, don't skitter your fly.

Behavior based on water movement

Water speed also affects the way a trout rises. This is independent of the type of insect (or other food) it is chasing. For example if a trout is holding in front of a rock where the breaking water speeds up around the structure, any adult insect that drifts by is going to speed up with the current. In this situation, even stationary insects look like they are escaping. This escaping food might bring an aggressive rise that would generally come from a trout chasing a skittering caddis or other highly active bug.

To simplify your approach, try to imagine what the trout sees as it is looking up at the water's surface while the silhouette of an insect drifts by. If the water is slick or slow moving, the silhouette of the fly will stay in the same plane or lane. So the trout will consume its food slowly because it does not appear to be escaping. If this same trout moves into a run with a seam or moving riffles, the reaction will be different. The silhouette of the fly will pop in and out of view as it rises and drops with the breaks in riffled runs. The fly will swirl out from a seam into slower water, making the image appear as if it is moving or trying to escape. So the fish will believe that it has to be aggressive before its food source disappears.

Take the time to identify the water the trout is feeding in and the trout's reaction. Observation is key when you are dealing with unique water flows, places where slow and fast water meet, or where water breaks around structure or objects in the river.

By nature, trout in rivers are relatively lazy when it comes to consuming their food. They hold in feeding lanes, waiting for the food to come to them. They will aggressively pursue a meal as long as they are replenishing the nutrients that were expended to catch the meal. In Alaska, one of the best top-water patterns is a mouse, because a hungry trout cannot pass up the protein supply of such a large source of food. Sometimes fish will abandon cover and oxygen requirements if there is an abundance of food. Use this to your advantage.

"Push out points" are areas where food is pushed into easy holding areas away from the current. Trout can feed here and not have to battle the current; instead, a trout will sit on the edge of the fast water and wait for its meal to be delivered. Imagine where the current would take an insect floating in the midcolumn of the river. That is where you will usually find the trout.

Dry-Fly Rigs

I prefer to fish two dry flies at one time because I can match different insects and imitate different stages of life. I only fish a single rig if the water I am fishing does not allow two flies. When choosing a fly, consider size (match the size of the insect, or go one size smaller) and silhouette. The next time you are shopping or tying dries, rotate the

Do not leave home in June or July without a good supply of Barr's Flashback PMD emergers. It is the most effective emerger to drop below a dry during the PMD hatch.

A Parachute Adams is one of the most effective mayfly imitations in the world. Like many great patterns, it produces great results, like this arctic grayling.

vise or turn the fly over and give it a good look from underneath. Patterns might look good to you in the fly bins, but it's what the trout thinks that is most important. Always consider what the fish sees when it looks up to the surface of the water. The view of the bottom of the fly looks radically different from this angle. Add in the sun, reflection from clouds, sunrises and sunsets, and the decision gets even more complicated. Look at a Griffith's Gnat—it certainly doesn't look like a midge to you or me, but it is deadly for trout feeding on midges.

I use fluorocarbon for fishing dry flies. The fact that fluorocarbon sinks doesn't make a difference with 5X and 6X tippets. I use 20 to 30 inches of tippet from the leader to the fly to keep the connection knot out of the trout's view, and from the lead fly to the trailing fly, I use 12 to 15 inches connected to the bend of the first fly's hook. I want the flies close enough that the fish can easily see both of them. I almost always choose a lead fly that imitates the adults on the surface, and change the trailing fly.

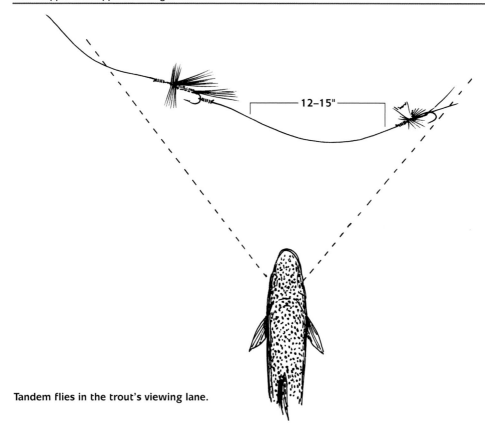

12–15"

Tandem flies in the trout's viewing lane.

My favorite rig is a dry fly with a PMD or BWO Barr Emerger. Other good emerger patterns are Gomez's Johnny Flash and RS2. Emerger patterns are so effective because they imitate a fly in the fish's comfort zone, just below the water's surface. Remember, when you see fish rising just under the surface, they are most likely feeding on emergers.

You can fish emergers at different depths, and they are effective from 2 inches to 24 inches under the surface. If you fish your emerger just under the surface, select an unweighted one and grease the tippet with floatant to about 2 inches before the emerger.

One variation of emerger is a floating nymph pattern. Since nymphs and emergers are such a familiar food source, when one is floating in the surface film, trout can't help but eat it. Trout feed on them because they don't have to break

the water's surface, leaving them less visible to predators from above. Most takes to a floating nymph will be a tip and sip—the trout tips its nose just above the water's surface to sip in the fly. When I see bulging rises, it's time to try a floating nymph.

Manufacturers sell special floating nymph patterns, but I usually just grease the tippet with fly floatant from the bend of the hook of the main fly all the way down to one inch shy of the nymph. That keeps the tippet material buoyant and floating on the surface, while the nymph remains in the film (or slightly below) in front of a regular, unweighted nymph. For instance, if Pale Morning Duns are the main food source on the water's surface, then I trail a PMD nymph below an imitation of an adult on top of the water's surface. Match the nymphal or pupating stage of the adult insect the trout is consuming.

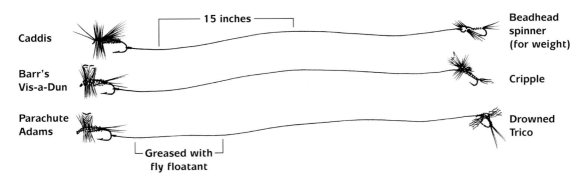

Caddis — 15 inches — Beadhead spinner (for weight)

Barr's Vis-a-Dun — Cripple

Parachute Adams — Drowned Trico

Greased with fly floatant

Control the depth to which your flies sink. Micro split shot can work, but may cause your flies to sink too fast. If you are fishing a single fly, grease the fluorocarbon tippet up to a few inches before the sinking dry. Fluorocarbon sinks, so the dry will ride in the film, or just below it. For a deeper presentation, use a wire body or a plastic bead so the fly will ride an inch or two below the surface.

Double dries are also effective, especially during a complex hatch where you may have six or more flies landing on the surface at one time—the most challenging dry-fly fishing there is. Two adult dries imitate several different mayflies and increase the chances of showing a fish something that it is looking for. One of my favorite rigs in the summer is a highly visible PMD dry with a Trico trailer. Don't forget that you can also fish drowned dries—which is especially effective for Tricos.

Not all insects enter the world looking perfect. Nor do they go through the hatching process or navigate tumultuous water unscathed. Bugs that are immobilized because of defects are called cripples, and trout, like all predators, key in on the weak.

I frequently fish a cripple behind a visible adult (or as the first fly) when the trout won't chase after the adults because they are flying away too quickly, or the fish don't want to expend the energy. In these situations, a pattern that imitates a deformed, immobilized insect often attracts fish. This can be so enticing that the fish are willing to move to the easy target.

Cripples are a great way to get trout to take on the surface when there are fluttering or escaping adults. Mike Lawson's PMD Cripple is one of the best patterns for imitating a bug that can't escape.

To fool wary trout, blend in with your surroundings. Don't get into the water unless you have to.

CHAPTER 9

Dry-Fly Casts and Presentations

Without question, the most exciting fishing is sight fishing to rising trout. There is nothing like the sharklike image of a trout breaking out of its underwater world to eat an insect on the water's surface. Sometimes it makes you weak in the knees, but to be successful you must have a calm, calculated approach. The faster you get into position, have your rig ready, and cast to the fish—minimizing all those false casts that waste time and spook fish—the better chance you have of the trout taking your fly.

When stalking fish, I get as close as possible. By getting close, I am more accurate and I can watch the fish's rises. Watching the rises tells me what they are feeding on, and I get a sense of their rhythm to time my cast. Two of my favorite short-game casts are the steeple cast punch and the sidearm cast.

The Steeple Cast Punch

With increased angling pressure, trout are warier these days. Leaders over 10 feet long are now common to prevent trout from detecting your line. This makes conventional casting with one or two dry flies a nightmare. Because the rod cannot load the line with only a few feet out of the tip, you hardly get any energy to deliver your flies to your target. To overcome this, I use a variation of the steeple cast, in which the rod stops high on the backcast (at one o'clock), allowing the small amount of line, leader, and tippet to unroll and straighten out. Then, on the forward casting stroke, I direct the fly line, leader, tippet, and flies at a 45-degree angle toward the water's surface. Apply some

force when you are forward casting at this angle so that the leader, tippet, and flies can straighten out: at this short distance there is not enough fly line to load the rod.

When using dry flies or flies with no weight, imagine punching the rod toward the water's surface. This straightens the leader, tippet, and flies before they land on the water, minimizing the surface disturbance. When using weighted nymphs or split shot, imagine that you are hammering a nail from the one o'clock rod position on the forward cast: this will allow your rig to straighten and land where you want it to.

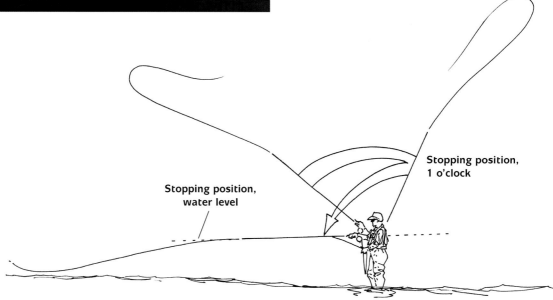

Stopping position, 1 o'clock

Stopping position, water level

The steeple cast is a great way to cast without taking the risk of false-casting. With a pick-up and lay-down, you can accurately place the flies above the trout. Important point: the fly is not crashing to the surface of the water. The goal is to cast toward the water, but have the fly line and leader unroll just before the fly gets there.

Sight fishing is close combat, so I find this cast essential, because I am able to cast my flies accurately with five feet or less of fly line out of the rod tip. I find it to be the most accurate cast in the wind, because there is not a lot of line to be blown off-course, and the tight loops cut through the wind. And this cast allows you to make a backcast high enough to go over any stream banks or bankside vegetation.

The Conventional False Cast

When you need more distance casting dry flies, use the conventional methods of a false cast with more than 10 feet of fly line out of the rod tip, and the rod stopping at 1 or 2 o'clock on the backcast and 10 or 11 o'clock on the forward stroke. While this cast is effective, the key to getting the most accuracy and power is a smooth acceleration to an abrupt stop.

With more two-fly rigs these days (a dry on top and a trailing emerger or cripple below), it is essential to keep them straight and separated in the water. Think of the backcast as a pull, and the forward stroke as a push. This helps you slow down and concentrate on each stroke, which in turn reduces false casts and produces more accurate deliveries. It is important to open your loops on both the back and forward casting strokes to prevent the flies from snagging the leader or fly line. The best way to achieve this is to allow the rod to drop slightly past the stopping point on the backcast; then after you stop on the forward cast, slightly drop your rod tip (point your thumb more toward the target).

Your rod tip must travel in a straight plane to cut through wind and make tighter loops, which allows the flies to straighten out instead of collapsing and bunching together on the water. Once you are comfortable with your casting, you can concentrate on the rising trout and you'll be confident that your delivery will be on the mark. Then you can focus on the trout and not the fly line in the air.

The Sidearm Cast

Casting overhead can spook fish. Pods of large trout lined the river's edge in calm, slick water during a trip to Montana's Missouri River, and I knew that if I false cast overhead from the boat, the entire pod would go down.

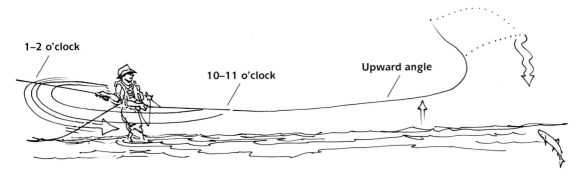

Sidearm cast. By kicking the rod up slightly at the end of the back- and forward-casting strokes, you gain two advantages: the leader is farther from the water during the pause of each stroke, preventing the lies or leader from ticking the water and spooking the trout. And the extra distance allows the fly to land softly on the water, making it appear more like a natural insect.

The Steeple Cast Punch

With minimal line out and the rod horizontally in front of you at water level, smoothly accelerate the rod up to a 12 o'clock position, accelerating to an abrupt stop. After the line has straightened out behind you and the rod loads, act like you are hammering down a nail, with your wrist straight, stopping the rod parallel to the water. The flex in your rod releases stored energy, forcing your flies to land in a straight line. This technique will ensure that the flies land in the same location every time you cast. JAY NICHOLS

The sidearm cast reduces the amount of rod movement overhead and works well for stealthy presentations to fish—even from a drift boat. PAT DORSEY

The sidearm cast uses the same principles as the conventional casting stroke. The rod should stop in front of you at 10 or 11 o'clock, and behind you at 1 or 2 o'clock. One of the biggest challenges an angler has when performing a sidearm false cast is ticking the water on the forward or back casting stoke, often putting a whole pod of feeding trout down. Compensate by giving your leader and line more distance from the water's surface at the end of each casting stroke. Keep the rod tip traveling on a straight path in the middle of each stroke. Then at the end, when you abruptly stop the rod, angle the rod tip up about six inches to send the line and leader upward. They will fall softly to the water's surface, with a little extra slack in the leader.

The Reach Mend

In the short game, you are fishing up close and making accurate casts. Since most of your casts will land a few feet above the trout, you don't have time for performing line-altering movements like mends. Instead, reach upstream during the forward part of your cast so that the fly line lands at a straight 45-degree angle from the flies to the rod tip. This will give you a long drag-free drift if you need it, without having to move your line once it is on the water.

Reach upstream after the line is unrolling half-way to the trout. Then drop your rod tip, to the left or right of your body, creating the 45-degree

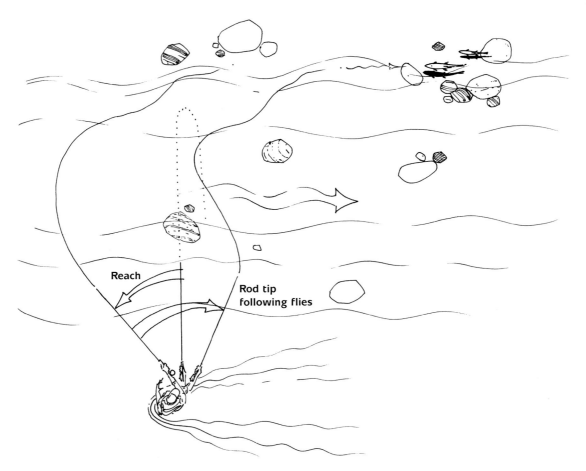

The reach mend. You can do this in tight quarters or in a low, tucked position by simply dropping the rod to the left or right of your body. If you extend your arm or reach out every time you drop the rod, you might spook the trout.

Wait for the fish to turn down on the fly when it takes from this position. Don't act too soon or you will pull the fly away from the fish before it actually takes.

approach to the flies. This is a great way to obtain a drag-free drift when you are sight fishing in close quarters. You keep tension on your flies, which allows you to adjust quickly if you need to.

Presentation

The angle of approach that you choose when fishing dry flies is determined by whether you want a dead drift or a more active presentation; whether the trout will spook; and limitations in wading or access, to mention just a few considerations. There are three main positions from which to cast.

Directly below the trout

Casting from below the trout has several advantages. You stay out of the fish's view, you can easily get a drag-free float, and it offers the best angle from which to hook the fish. When you cast below the trout and add an angle of 45 degrees, you simply lift straight up every time the fish eats, and you hook more trout directly in the corner of the mouth. Make sure to control line by stripping it back in as the flies drift back to you.

Above the trout

From upstream of the trout, you can present your flies with a natural drag-free drift by adding "S" curves in your cast. Your line and leader will look like a slithering snake when they land on the water. To put S curves in your presentation casts, stop the rod at 10 or 11 o'clock on the forward casting stroke. Then as your rod releases the stored energy from the flex and your line begins to unroll in front of you, make three or four side-to-side movements with the rod tip as the line moves forward. Keep the left-to-right movements of the rod tip to 24 inches or less so that you don't redirect the line and flies. In this presentation, the fly approaches the fish before the leader. The risk is that the fly line will float into the trout's viewing

The S-curve Cast

To make S curves in your line, move the rod tip about a foot, side to side, after you stop the rod on the forward casting stroke. This will create winding curves in your line by the time it lands on the water, giving you a long, drag-free drift. JAY NICHOLS

1

The Curve Cast

To create a curve in your line: on the forward cast the line unrolls in front of you. Roll your wrist upstream of the trout as the line straightens out. This will create a U-shaped loop of line upstream of the fish. After the rig has landed, there will be a curve in your line, and the flies will be the first thing visible to the trout. JAY NICHOLS

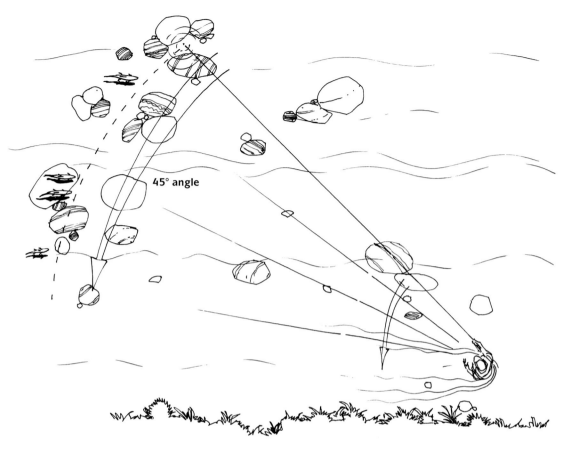

45° angle

The swing presentation. Cast your flies far enough upstream of the trout that they swing in front of the fish in the middle of its viewing lane. If you overshoot, pull in line or take a step back. It is critical that the flies swing in front of the fish and not over their backs. How far above the fish you cast depends on the water temperature and the depth of the fish. In three or four feet of water, I like to swing the fly about six inches in front of the fish.

lane. With a long leader and presentations from a 45-degree angle, you can make many casts without drag to feeding fish. Be sure to wait until the flies drift past the trout before you pick up and recast, to prevent disturbance on the water that might spook the fish.

When you are imitating a moving food source on the water's surface, cast above the trout, keeping your line taut while the fly drifts downstream and swings in front of the trout's viewing lane. To swing your flies when you are at a 45-degree angle to the trout, keep the rod tip low, and gradually move the

tip toward the bank. The flies will swing as they follow the rod.

The 45-degree angle is important so that when the fish does eat your fly, you can set the hook by sweeping your rod to the side of the river you are positioned on. Wait until the trout has consumed the fly and his head is back below the surface before setting the hook.

Across-stream from the trout
When you are across-stream, or perpendicular, to a trout, there are many ways to present the fly.

With the overhanging tree for protection, the trout in this side channel were not wary and were happily rising to the surface. I could get close to them without spooking them. I probably would have snagged the tree if I tried to make presentations from above or below the trout. JAY NICHOLS

The most common is the traditional pick-up and lay-down, applying a mend for a drag-free drift, or no mend if you want the flies to skitter along the surface. I use a curve cast to place the fly directly above the fish and the fly line in a curve upstream of the trout. The fish will see the fly first, and the line is out of its window. This cast gives you a natural drag-free drift without applying an on-water mend, and it is perfect when you need to drift to a fish in fast water. At a short distance, you don't have time to make a mend after your line has landed on the water. And if you are fishing around obstacles like rocks or logjams and you need to reach the trout, a curve cast can wrap your flies and leader around the object, allowing you to get a presentation, even if it is brief, to a feeding fish.

Trout rise both sporadically and steadily. When a trout rises three times or more in one minute, I consider it an actively feeding fish. If the rises are two or fewer times in a minute, I classify it as sporadic. Sporadic risers are difficult to entice if there are few naturals present. If there are many adults on the water and you see a trout occasionally break the surface with a minute or more passing by between each take, the trout is probably eating something below the surface, or it may simply be resting after heavy feeding activity.

Sections of turbulent water are often overlooked by anglers, but highly-oxygenated water attracts fish, so don't pass them by without a look.

Nymphing Presentations and Casts

When I first started nymphing, I learned how to achieve a natural, drag-free drift, and how to read water so that I could effectively cover a run. These techniques and concepts are the building blocks to successful fishing.

Many anglers are proficient at nymphing with an indicator, and rely on the strike indicator to tell them when a fish has taken the fly. This, in my opinion, is a disadvantage. It is too easy to be comfortable with dead-drifting—wondering where your fly will drift next time it passes through the run, instead of locating the trout and casting right to it. This dead-drifting complacency keeps you from taking your subsurface fishing to the next level. The best indicator is the trout itself—not the indicator on your leader. Take nymphing one step further: strive to sight-fish to a trout, and rely on the fish's movements to know when to set the hook. There is nothing like watching a fish race over to your fly, open up its white mouth, and slam it.

The more accurate you are, and the fewer false casts or movements you create from above, the better off you are. The goal is to make every drift count. For the most accurate casts, keep tension on the fly or flies as they drift. I estimate that 70 percent of the presentations I make to a trout are not drifting drag free. Tension on the line lets you control the flies as they drift, and allows

Suspended fish feed heavily on emergers.

John Barr holds a trout that he caught in a deep run. Trout blend in well with the river bottom, so the key to finding trout is to locate the silhouette of a fish.

you to adjust the length of line quickly before your rig reaches the trout. You can adjust to different situations, and the flies remain in a straight line every time you present them. Don't rely on slack line to get the imitations into the trout's viewing lane: turbulence in the water might redirect your flies elsewhere. I am not saying that a drag-free drift is not useful in some situations. But it can be the wrong approach to a trout in close quarters. Keep some tension on the line so that the flies will drift right where you want them to go.

The Downstream Drift

The best way to present a fly to a wary trout in both shallow, clear water, and slow-moving, deep water is from upstream, at a 45-degree angle to your target. Every cast you make keeps you, the fly line, and any unnatural objects upstream and out

of the trout's viewing lane. The first thing the fish will see will be your flies. However, it can be difficult to get into position and cast without spooking the fish. Be sure to stay far enough upstream, keep a low profile, and stay out of view. My good friend John Barr prefers to feed the flies to the trout from upstream. Here is what he has to say about it.

"Nearly forty years ago, while fishing Nelson's Spring Creek, George Anderson introduced me to sight-nymphing. He would locate a fish, get upstream of it, and then cast a weighted nymph above the fish, dead-drifting the fly into the fish's face. He taught me to watch the fish, and if the mouth opened and showed white or if the fish moved slightly, he would set the hook. More often than not, he was tight to a trout.

"Through the years, I have successfully applied this relatively simple approach countless times in

John Barr fights a trout after a downstream delivery using the Hopper-Copper-Dropper method. After a hard-fought battle, he landed the Yampa River wild rainbow.

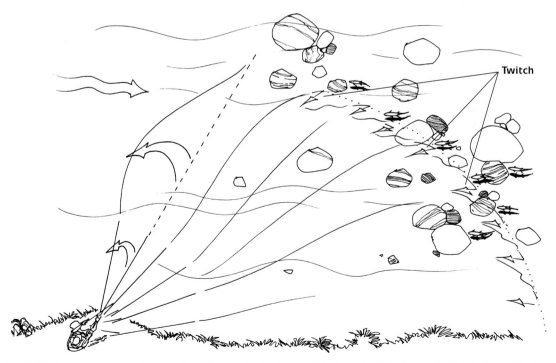

Twitch

Dead-drifting streamers. Twitch the fly without stripping it out of the lane that it is drifting in. Pull in 6 to 12 inches of line periodically during the drift, then immediately let the same amount back through the rod tip, keeping the fly traveling in a straight line. The streamer will pulsate and wiggle, resembling a wounded baitfish.

many different fisheries. If the situation presents it-self (sometimes you cannot see the fish and you must blind-fish the likely holding areas), there is no better way to hook trout and to be able to pick out the larger fish. The mistake many anglers make is they only blind-fish the obvious runs and never look for fish. Between the obvious runs, there are slight depressions and other habitat that can hold fish. The water between the pools often contains riffles, making it more difficult for the fish to de-tect your presence, allowing you to position your-self and present your fly without spooking the fish.

"The depth and speed of the water, and how deep the fish is holding, will determine how much weight you need and where you cast to get the fly into the fish's face. I usually use two or three nymphs, with a heavy top nymph, to get the often unweighted pattern on the bottom down to the fish. The deeper the fish is holding, the farther above the fish I will cast, which allows the nymphs time to sink to the fish's level. I avoid split shot, which can hinge the leader, producing an unnatu-ral drift and spooking pressured fish.

"I never set unless I see a white mouth or move-ment so as to avoid foul-hooking fish. Whether sight-fishing or blind-fishing, you are going to foul-hook some fish. If you do foul-hook a fish and you cannot land it quickly, you should break it off.

"Sight fishing is obviously not the only way to successfully fish, but it is an approach that all fly fishermen should keep in mind to make a day on the river more fun and productive."

One advantage to this high-angled position is that you can manipulate the flies as they drift. If the trout is feeding, you can maneuver a drag-free drift to the trout. Or you can swing the flies to the fish, causing it to move or strike. One thing to re-member is that whether you have tension in your line or a slack line, you can still achieve a dead drift. Without slack, the drift will remain dead for a shorter period than it would if you provide slack from a mend.

The Fly Slap

Make sure your flies are clean. If they have de-bris on them, fish won't eat them.

The traditional way of cleaning your flies is to physically pick them up and meticulously clean them, taking away precious fishing time. The fly slap is a fast, effective, albeit not a graceful, way of cleaning your flies. It is a simple technique that keeps your flies in the water longer.

It's a simple technique: With a foot or two of fly line out of the rod tip, rotate your arm, and slap the flies a few times on the water downstream of the trout. Keep tension on the line throughout the ro-tation, and every time the flies hit the water, pull back and up, continuing the motion. The slapping motion cleans the flies. It's the best way to keep your flies free of vegetation—no fumbling while you grab your leader, tippet, or flies, and no spook-ing the trout. Then you can easily present the flies after the slap has cleared your rig downstream of the trout.

The fly slap. Point your rod downstream from where you are positioned. If the trout is too close you can move carefully downstream with your rod in a straight downstream position. Then with a stiff arm, perform a continuous roll with the fly slapping the water with each new rotation. If your arm is not straight, the line will collapse and lose energy. Keep constant tension on your leader, tippet, and line: the flies will skip across the surface on every pass, and after three or four swipes, you are ready to cast with clean flies.

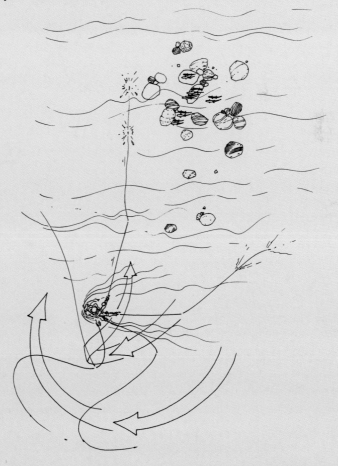

Presentation after the slap

If there is fair amount of space between you and your target, slack in the line will be an advantage because the flies will drift easier. When you are close to the fish, tension is helpful achieving a dead drift; you are more accurate from a short distance, and the drift is often shorter, so you don't need a lot of slack to achieve the right presentation.

Another favorite technique is the twitch, where I twitch the rod tip, pausing occasionally between twitches, so the nymphs or emergers dart across the run. Or I wait until the fly is in front of the trout and twitch a few times to dance the fly. This is great for enticing wary trout or fish that are casually feeding in a shallow run.

When you are positioned above a trout and swing your flies downstream, across, and in front of the trout's viewing lane, you may need another foot of line. It is hard to adjust accurately without overextending the line, so here is a tip: if you have a size twelve shoe, look down at your feet and move one step forward. This gets you about one foot closer to the fish without the guesswork. Sometimes moving only six inches makes a difference.

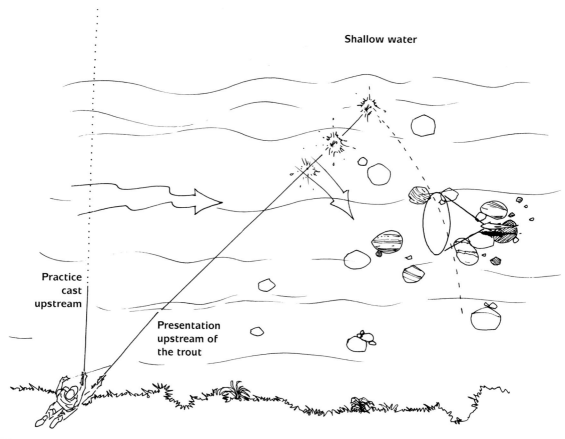

Think short. When you are above the trout and casting into shallow water, make a practice cast directly across stream and far away from the trout to gauge your distance. Then cast beyond the fish and keep tension on the flies so they will drift and swing downstream. The goal is to keep the flies upstream of the fish so that you don't snag it, but still get the flies close enough so that the fish sees them. Adjust the length of line by stripping line in or feeding line out.

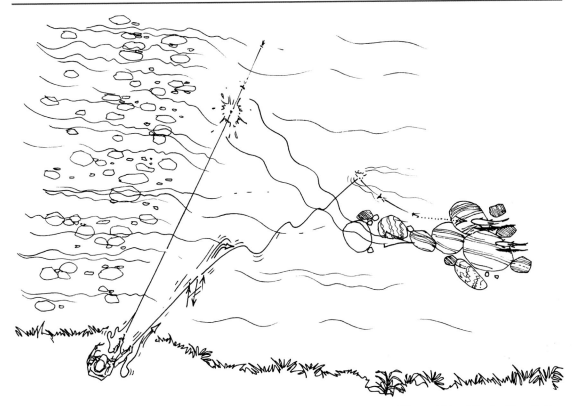

Deep water drifts. To cast downstream to a fish in deep water, the key is to feed line quickly while the flies, fly line, and strike indicator remain in a straight line. You can do this by kicking the rod up one or two feet while it is horizontal to the water and your line is drifting downstream. This line movement will create mends and you can extend the drift to the trout.

Adjusting for water depth

In shallow water drifts, it is hard to keep from snagging the river bottom. Snags spook the trout because pulling the rig free disturbs the water. Swing drifts or moving flies in shallow runs will keep your rig off the bottom. This also gives you more control of the drift and may trigger a strike when the flies swing in front of the trout.

When you drift to the fish, keep your flies just above or slightly to the side of the trout—preferably on the side where you are standing. This will keep your flies from rubbing or snagging the trout if it does not eat on the first or second drift. If you are off, instead of picking up your flies to recast and maybe spooking the fish, your flies to recast and maybe spooking the fish, simply strip in line (or feed line out) to compensate.

It is important to develop accurate, systematic presentations. For example, when a client and I are casting short distances to trout that we can see, I teach my client how to perform the tension cast correctly, step-by-step. If you have a systematic approach for each situation, you will build your confidence and catch more fish.

For deep-water drifts downstream to the trout, give the flies time to sink and maintain that depth until they reach the fish. Do this by feeding a predetermined amount of line to the trout. Only mend when you need to, or when the line is about to drag. Make sure the flies stay in a straight line, one foot to either side of the trout: close enough so that the fish can see your flies, but because they are not in line with the fish, they will not snag it.

To determine the proper amount of line, I make a practice cast upstream away from the trout.

This big rainbow didn't hesitate to move two feet and slam the nymph as it swung through its viewing lane.

When presenting a fly from a perpendicular position, get close to the water's surface and out of view. In this case, the angler is disguised by the high bank behind him.

Once I think the length across river is the same distance I need to reach the trout, I strip in the excess line, leaving enough line out of the rod tip to make the cast and start the drift. With the flies in a straight line, I keep the rod tip low above the water's surface, to prevent any movement that the trout might see. When I need to feed line, I simply kick the rod tip up a few feet and let the line shoot out. This delivers a drag-free drift without spooking the trout, and I maintain line control.

You can also move your flies, which works well for fish feeding on caddis and other moving bugs. Let the line drag at the end of the swing, or lift the rod tip as the fly reaches the trout, to imitate a rising pupa or diving adult caddis.

The Perpendicular Presentation

The most rewarding part of sight fishing with subsurface flies is watching the trout kick side-to-side or up-and-down as it takes. The best way to see these movements is from an angle perpendicular or slightly downstream of the trout. You are close to the fish, and the movements are more visible than they would be if you were upstream or downstream. You learn so much from

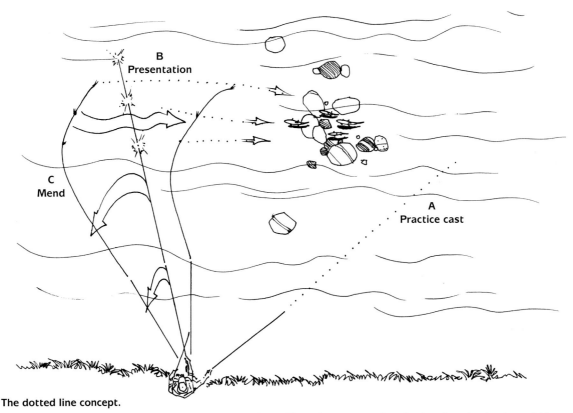

The dotted line concept.

A. Measure the distance downstream of the trout. You will need to cast one foot farther than the depth at which the trout is holding. Cast at a 45-degree angle to the fish.

B. The splash of your split shot should land directly upstream of the fish.

C. Mend your line to help your flies sink. Don't make a large mend. The weight, leader, and line will be the first things the trout sees. The split shot should be directly upstream of the trout. With practice, you can make a reach mend as you cast.

their feeding behavior; you will set the hook 70 percent of the time before the indicator even moves. Makes you wonder just how many strikes you missed when the trout took the fly and spit it out before you even knew. Now the guessing game is done.

From this angle, use the dotted-line technique. This is a systematic approach that assures you that the trout will see every drift. Make an imaginary line upstream, just past where your flies will land, at a 45-degree angle to the trout. The trick to this presentation is twofold: You must measure your

cast beforehand and make a final presentation cast in which your rod, line, and leader remain out of the trout's view. When the flies hit the water, mend your line, leader, indicator, and weight upstream of the trout. The first thing the trout sees is your flies.

The goal is to control the flies as they drift naturally back toward the bank you are standing on. Do this by keeping tension on the flies, even after you have mended the line, placing it above the flies. Make sure your presentation is slightly short of the trout as it drifts downstream, allowing the

Binoculars are a great way to view trout—especially trout rising at a distance or across-stream. They let you watch feeding behavior without spooking the fish.

fish a chance to turn and take the fly without lining or spooking.

Six inches can make or break your presentation, so start short and allow the trout to turn and take the fly. This prevents foul-hooking the trout and lets you make many drifts without the fish suspecting anything unnatural. It is the movement of your feet and body rather than the line that ensures accuracy. For example, if you are directly across-stream from a trout, and you make a presentation that is ten inches too far, look down at your size ten boot and take one step back. Your feet are a great point of reference because you know how many inches your boot is. It is much easier to adjust by moving—pulling line out or stripping it back in is a complete guessing game. Such a simple "step" can make all the difference.

When you are across from the trout, eliminate as much false casting as possible. To reduce motions, make your false casts out of view of your target, downstream of the trout. When you are ready to make a presentation, pause slightly longer on the last backcast to allow the line to straighten out, and so that you can redirect the line easier on the forward casting stroke. Then lay the flies down above the trout. Keep the same amount of line out with every presentation to increase your accuracy. Remember to stay low—whether that is hunching your shoulders, crouching on one knee, or even crawling on all fours—so that the trout does not detect you.

Downstream

To scan the river looking for trout, walk upriver approaching the trout from its backside where it has a blind spot in its viewing window. You can scan a larger section of river and you have time to decide from which angle you should fish. This is my least favorite approach because there is a high risk that the fish will see some part of your rig before it sees the fly, and it may spook.

From downstream, you can deliver the flies in two ways. The first way is from an angle where the cast and flies land upstream at a 45-degree angle to the trout. The second is from directly below the trout. Each way has its own advantages, and having additional ways to present the flies will lead to more hookups.

Upstream 45-degree Presentation

The safest cast to make to the trout above you is at a 45-degree angle. This keeps everything out of view, and it prevents the fly line from landing or moving above the trout. In this situation, I make a false cast, or I pick up and lay down across-stream or below the fish, to determine the right distance. Then I cast above the trout. How far you need to place the flies above the fish depends on how deep the trout is. For shallow water, two or three feet is usually enough; deep water can require four or more feet.

Once the fly lands, be sure to gain line quickly enough to keep slack out of the line. Be sure to maintain tension so that you can strike or adjust the fly's position. Apply a small mend toward the river's edge you are casting from. Mend your fly line closer to the flies and leader to place the fly line out of the trout's viewing lane.

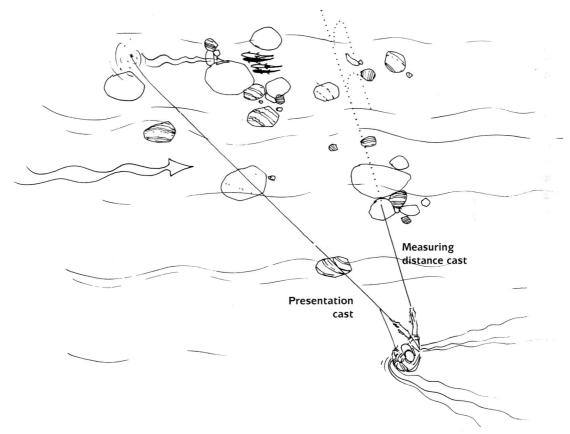

Measuring distance cast

Presentation cast

Upstream and out of view. Don't false cast over the fish: the shadow or water from your line might spook it. Instead, get below the fish at a 45-degree angle. Work out enough line to cover the distance between you and the fish, measuring about one or two extra feet. On your delivery, aim for one to three feet above the fish, in the same seam or current that the fish is feeding in.

When you present to a trout that is directly above you, remember to stay low. Extend the length of your leader to prevent trout from detecting your line.

The easiest part of this presentation is setting the hook. Because you are already downstream of the fish, lift your rod vertically to set the hook. From the other positions, either perpendicular or upstream, it is more difficult to be sure that the fly is in the corner of the trout's jaw. If you are downstream, the hook will go the right direction.

When you cast upstream at a 45-degree angle above the trout, the key is to prevent your flies from rubbing the trout's body, and to keep your split shot or something unnatural from being detected. To do this, cast slightly to the right or left of the trout, not directly above the fish: the flies will land in the trout's viewing lane and then gradually drift slightly to the right or the left of the fish. The fish will see your flies and the rig won't rub the trout's body. Remember to keep tension on your flies, leader, and fly line while they drift downstream.

Presenting Directly Below the Trout

Sometimes you are in a tight spot and cannot cast from a 45-degree angle. You might have to deliver the flies to the trout from directly below the target. In my opinion, this is the worst-case scenario.

I see many anglers try this presentation, not recognizing the effect they are having on both the fish and the surrounding water. Sure, you can cast a straight line into the trout's feeding lane, but do you know for sure that the direction the water is flowing will keep your flies moving in a straight line? With multiple current seams, speeds, and structures in the river, there are so many reasons that the water may not be flowing evenly that this position is difficult to predict. Most importantly, without an extremely long leader, it's hard to get the flies above the trout without spooking the fish. This is why I would rank this positioning as a D, and revert back to A, B, or C for a better grade.

It is difficult to cast undetected. Consider the difficulties: In deep water, the trout's viewing lane is wide and vast. On the other hand, in shallow water the fish are wary because they don't have the security of deep water, so your line is detected more easily.

In deep water, an aerial mend helps—simply drop the rod tip to one side as your line is unrolling in front of you. Or apply a stack mend by throwing a small loop of extra fly line to either side of the trout, moving the fly line and indicator out of the trout's viewing lane. This keeps your flies drag-free, allowing them to sink without spooking the trout with your fly line or indicator.

In shallow water or in close quarters, I remove my strike indicator and rely on the trout to tell me when to set. You want to be able to control the sinking rate of your flies as they pass by the trout. Always start light so you do not snag bottom and spook the trout. The main goal is to let only the leader land above the trout and to never let your fly line come into the fish's view.

Line Control

Anglers often have too much line out. While blind fishing, or fishing while reading runs, they may have excess line out for big mends and extended drifts. But in most sight-fishing situations, you have to cast to a different spot in the river every time.

For example, if you cast to a trout ten feet away and you target the trout's viewing lane, you may have fifteen feet of line out. Every time you pick up to recast, you run the risk of over-shooting the trout. The line might go ten feet on one drift and twelve or more on the next. In this example, the trout may only see one presentation for every five. Try to determine the distance downstream of the

It is important to learn good casting habits—the sooner the better. Madelyn Mayer is making her daddy proud.

The Arm Roll Cast

1. To start the arm roll cast, load the rod from the tension of the line off the water's surface. Continue at an upward forty-five degree angle to get the maximum flex, storing energy in the rod.

2. When the leader, flies, and tippet are clear of the water, allow the fly line to unroll while you start the rolling rotation of your arm. Keep your forearm and wrist straight.

3. Roll your arm down to the side upstream of the trout. This will continue the casting stroke and prevent the trout from detecting the fly line.

4. Allow the line to unroll in front of you while you drop the rod tip to your upstream side.

5. The result is a proper presentation with a reach mend above the trout. This eliminates the need to mend, avoids disturbing the water, and eliminates any movement above the trout.

Line management is critical for accuracy. Only cast the amount of line that you need to reach the fish, and make minor adjustments by stepping forward or backward.

trout, and once you get it right, stick with it. Every cast should count.

Try to prevent bad habits, like pulling a little bit of line out with every cast. The flies will land in a different location every time you make a presentation because you are constantly extending the length of fly line. Keep your left hand on the line while your right hand moves the rod (or the other way around if you are a lefty).

Another bad habit is stopping the rod too high. This can prevent your flies from landing in a straight line on the water: the high arc on the forward cast resembles a throwing motion, which shocks the leader, and makes it land awkwardly on the water's surface. You've lost control of where the flies land.

If you have to strip line in while you drift through a run, keep the same amount of line out for each cast and retrieve. If you stop the rod close to the water's surface, the flies will straighten out and land in the same target area above the trout. If you need more distance, instead of pulling line out of your reel, reposition your body. You will be more accurate.

In addition to controlling the length of your line, you must control what happens to the line after you set on the fish. Many anglers place the fly line under their index finger to control it, and so that they know where it is if they need to strip line in or pull more line out. But if you are perpendicular to the trout and you do not need to feed or strip line, don't hold the line under your index finger. Allow the reel to apply the pressure if the trout bolts; that reduces the risk of the trout breaking off because you pinched the line. This is the biggest advantage to line control in shallow water—you will get more fish in the net with fewer break-offs. I can't count the number of times I've seen anglers lose trout to an LDR (lost down river) because of a slight hesitation to release the line from under their fingers. A small adjustment and this simple technique can make all the difference in landing trout.

The Casts

In narrow waterways, most casts to trout feeding below the surface will be made with little or no fly line out of the rod tip. This makes it important to cast using more arm movements than by loading the rod and swinging it through the greatest arc. Using arm movements will allow your flies to land in a straight line, making you more accurate. When you do this correctly, you can hit the same spot every time without the fly line or leader going over the trout, and you will get more drifts to the trout.

I use the following two casts on a regular basis to eliminate tangles and missed opportunities. They both use two flies, split shot, and an indicator.

Arm roll cast

The arm roll eliminates false casting above the trout. The cast helps you keep tension on the fly or flies, which helps you load the rod at short distances and place the fly in the same location each time. You can perform this cast with three feet or thirty feet of line out of the tip.

Start with your rod tip at the surface of the water, pointing downstream. Then keeping your arm straight, bring your arm in an upward rolling motion on the backcast. Continuing the roll through the forward stroke, ending at the water's surface where you want your flies to go. To complete the cast, add a reach before the rod tip stops at the water's surface on the forward cast. This works well in fast moving water when you are rapidly presenting a fly to a fish without the time to mend. The cast is simple, and it is the most effective way I have found to present the flies to wary trout.

Tension cast

The tension cast is effective for casting quickly from a low position while you are moving upstream. The line hangs in the water because of the tension of the fly line on the water's surface, and that loads the rod. It is effective up to about twenty feet.

To perform the cast, place the rod at a 10 or 11 o'clock position (depending on how high or low your body is), and at a 45-degree angle down-

stream. Turn your wrist so that the bottom of the reel is facing the trout. For the forward stroke: take your rod from the 10 or 11 o'clock position, keep your wrist straight, and power-stop at the water's surface. The tension from the fly line on the water's surface will flex and load the rod, shooting your flies and fly line upstream to land in a straight line above the target.

I use this cast over all others when I am searching water while walking, because the line is already hanging in the water, creating the tension to load the rod as I am moving upstream. So there is only one motion left to make a presentation to the trout: the forward motion of the casting stroke to present the fly.

Depth-Finding System

When you sight-fish in deep water you need to know where your flies are drifting in relation to where the trout is holding. You need a depth-finding system.

You can control the sink rate to cover different water depths with numerous drifts. Develop a tier system that lets you add weight with a split shot or weighted fly to work your way down to where the trout are feeding. Always start light: that gives the fish a chance to move up in the water column to take your fly. Add and remove split shot to adjust your depth.

Try to get your flies in front of the trout within one or two casts. However, because you are trying to determine how deep the trout is, you can't always do this quickly. Don't rush the situation by over-weighting your rig and thereby snagging or spooking the fish because you are too deep. Instead, start light, or above, the fish, and then gradually work your way down. The trout will have the opportunity to rise in the water column to take the fly, and you won't lose the target altogether.

The Tension Cast

1. At the end of your drift, lift the rod to 10 o'clock and pause. The pause creates tension that will later load the rod. JAY NICHOLS

2. From this still position, turn your wrist so that the rod tip and the bottom of the reel are pointing toward the fish. Begin a forward-casting motion toward the water's surface.

3. Continue driving the rod tip toward the water with force as your line and leader unroll.

4. Lower the rod tip until the rod is horizontal and pointed in the direction of the cast. The line will straighten out in the air.

5. When the fly line, leader, tippet, and flies are straight, gradually drop the rod tip to the water's surface. This results in a fast, effective, tension cast—placing your flies above the target every time.

A good pattern is versatile. Greg Garcia's Rojo Midge imitates an emerging midge or, with the tuft cut off, a midge larva.

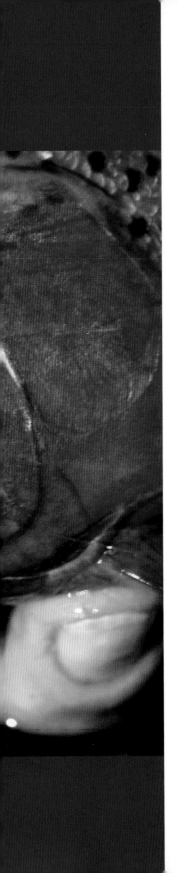

CHAPTER 11

Nymph Rigs and Patterns

Sight fishing with nymphs and emergers takes the thrill of fly fishing up another notch. The visual thrill you get with dry flies makes a whole day on the water a great hunting experience.

Most of the rigs that I use are two-fly setups attached by fluorocarbon. There are many advantages to using two flies. The first advantage is that you can imitate two different insects on one rig or imitate two different stages of the insect's life cycle (for example, the fly closest to the weight resembles a nymph and the fly farthest from the weight imitates an emerger).

The second advantage is that you can cover different depths in the water. The first fly remains in the bottom column, and a second, lightly-weighted or nonweighted fly floats higher. And you can cover more water with two flies. For example, if you are fishing a long, riffled run with multiple trout visibly feeding throughout the width of the water, using one fly means more casts to each trout. With two flies, 18 inches or more apart, you can cover more water (both in the water column and across the stream).

I rig the first fly to the eye of the hook, using a clinch knot on small flies (size 22 to 18), and an improved clinch knot for larger flies and tippet. I use the improved clinch knot only on larger flies because the tippet will reach the breaking point before the knot gives way. Moreover, the smaller the knot, the less visible and more natural the nymph or emerger will look to the trout.

To connect the second piece of tippet to the second fly, use a clinch knot on the bend of the first fly's hook. This prevents tangles better than connect-

Brown trout are notorious for holding in the cover of deep runs. Adjust your rig to get your flies down to them.

If you are comfortable tying knots, you can re-rig quickly and use different setups to meet different conditions. JAY NICHOLS

ing the fly through the eye of the hook, and it gives a more horizontal drift through the water, making the silhouette more visible to the trout. While there are many knots you can use to connect a two-fly rig, it is important to have confidence in your rig. Practice with your rig in different water conditions.

Two-Fly Rigs with Split Shot

Split shot is an effective way to get your flies deep when you need to get deep quickly. Start by applying a small amount of weight first and then if you need to get deeper in the water, add another piece of shot. After using split shot regularly, you will develop a tier system in which you know the size of the shot you need to get as deep as you need to.

Size of split shot is determined by numbers or letters. For example, one variety of shot is labeled

0 (the largest) and 6 (the smallest). With experience, you will know what number shot will get you to the trout's depth. However, if you are not sure, instead of chunking deep and risking a snag, you can start with #4 or #2 shot, and add more if you need to. This effective tier system allows you to reach the right depth.

A common two-fly rig is a 9-foot or longer leader attached to two pieces of tippet, each 18 inches or longer. Place a split shot an inch above the surgeon's knot to prevent the split shot from fraying and weakening the connection knot. Above the split shot, place a strike indicator, preferably white or tan to resemble foam or scum on the water's surface.

I like to increase the length of leader from ten to fifteen feet to prevent the trout from detecting the fly line. Increasing the leader length also allows you to adjust the placement of the strike

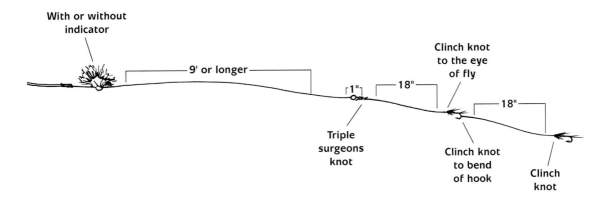

With or without indicator

9' or longer

Clinch knot to the eye of fly

1"

18"

18"

Triple surgeons knot

Clinch knot to bend of hook

Clinch knot

Two-fly rig with split shot and indicator. When I rig weights with two flies and an indicator, I keep the distance between two flies approximately the same each time I rig. My tippet length is a consistent eighteen inches. This allows me to be precise because the distance from the split shot is the same every time I cast. When I place the strike indicator, I never go less than four feet. This keeps the unnatural object out of the trout's viewing lane.

indicator when you are fishing a different water depth. Be sure that the leader and tippet are non-light-reflecting fluorocarbon.

This is an ideal setup for deep water, when you need to get down to a trout but you cannot easily detect feeding movements. In dirty water with low visibility, an indicator helps you know when a trout has taken your fly. You can adjust your strike indicator to help suspend the flies in deep water, so you will see more takes even when it is difficult to see into the water. Remember to keep it four feet or more away from the split shot to prevent the trout from seeing it. A strike indicator used this way should be called a suspender because the strike indicator is primarily suspending the flies in the water column, preventing them from snagging bottom.

Weighted Flies with No Split Shot

If fish are wary, split shot decreases your catch rate. Trout sometimes see the split shot. This is particularly true in clear water or when hunting trophy trout. Instead of split shot, consider using weighted flies.

John Barr's Tungstone is a great pattern to use instead of split shot. The tungsten bead and lead wrapped on the body gets the fly deep quickly and sinks your rig.

Forever Fluorocarbon

Angling pressure has made trout more wary these days. At even the slightest hint of something unnatural, trout will let your imitation drift by without even a look. The big advantage of fluorocarbon is that it reflects less light than monofilament nylon, giving you the upper hand. Because it is nearly invisible, I only use fluorocarbon for dry flies and subsurface patterns.

Fluorocarbon is stronger and more abrasion-resistant than monofilament. The knots connecting it to fluorocarbon or monofilament need to be strong. When I connect a leader to a tippet, I use a triple surgeon's knot instead of a double for the extra strength. Most believe fluorocarbon is not as buoyant as monofilament, but that is not as important when you are using small diameters (7X to 5X). Only on heavier lines, 4X and above, does this become a factor.

I carry 6X through 3X fluorocarbon tippets and leaders. For selective trout, I downsize my tippet to one size smaller than the leader.

The best way to add weight to a fly is by wrapping lead underneath the material of the fly, or—my favorite—by tying a tungsten bead behind the hook eye. I prefer the bead weight because it is similar to the split-shot-tier system technique. Start with light flies for the first presentations and, if you are not deep enough, you can re-tie a fly with a larger bead to reach the trout's depth. In addition, if the trout are keying in on a certain color on that specific day, you can match the bead to that color.

To a 9-foot leader, attach about 18 inches of tippet with a triple surgeon's knot. To that tippet, clinch knot the first fly, attach 18 inches of tippet to the bend of the first fly, and then attach your second fly.

The first fly will act like a piece of shot, hugging the bottom of the run or floating midcolumn. To cover different depths, trail a lighter fly off the back of the lead fly. Or use weight on both flies to drift at the same depth. This is a great setup for deep runs in the winter and early spring when flows are typically low and clear and trout inspect your flies.

When I use weighted flies I use one fly with weight and one fly without. For deep water, and situations when the trout are near the bottom, I weight the bottom fly to get my flies deep, into the trout's viewing lane. When trout are suspended or in shallow water, I weight the lead fly and leave the trailing fly unweighted, allowing it to drift midcolumn in the river while the main fly (with weight) is drifting toward the river bottom. By weighting only the first fly, you present to the trout in different water depths without worrying about two weighted flies snagging the river bottom.

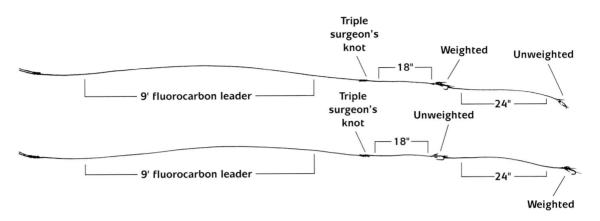

Two-fly rigs, weighted and unweighted flies on bottom. Use a 9-foot leader. I locate the first fly 18 inches from the surgeon's knot and the trailing fly 24 inches from the lead fly. This gives me the distance to drift at different water depths, whether the weighted fly is the first or the second fly.

Hopper, Copper, Dropper

We have all been there: drifting flies to a trout you can see suspended in the run, a trout that is feeding heavily. Then all of a sudden the fish rushes up and crashes the indicator. You react by setting the hook, knowing there is no chance of hooking the trout. You find yourself muttering, "Man, I should have had a hopper on for an indicator." Well, this rig is your chance at redemption. This is for all those surprise takes you never expect.

Suspended in a run are feeding fish—the ideal setting for a trout to hold in when you are sight-fishing. You have some breathing room to find the correct depth. The fish can move up, down, or from side-to-side to take the fly. In these situations, fish might spook when they see an indicator (even a white one), since they are close to the water's surface.

Increase your odds with three flies. You can imitate three stages of life with dry flies, emergers, and nymphs. A hopper makes your rig look completely natural without the unnatural strike indicator spooking the trout. Over the last four years, I've had great success with the Hopper, Copper, Dropper rig. The fly drifts in the midcolumn of

every run, and there is no risk of snagging the bottom. Trout have a chance to look it over, and they often like what they see.

To rig this three-fly approach, concentrate on the size of the leader and tippet material, ensuring that the flies will turn over but not tangle. Use a 3X to 4X fluorocarbon leader for the hopper. This is stiff enough to turn the hopper over and prevent the leader from spinning. Then determine the depth you need, and match it with the length of 4X to 5X fluorocarbon tippet material for the Copper John. A safe depth is usually three to four feet, depending on how deep the run is. For very shallow water setups, trail the Copper only a foot below the Hopper, giving the trout a chance at top and bottom takes in the run. When the water is this shallow, drop only one fly below the Hopper so that you don't snag the bottom.

For the final fly, use a piece of 5X to 6X tippet, placed 12 to 18 inches below the Hopper. Use one of John Barr's most effective and popular patterns, the BWO or PMD Barr's Emerger. I use a Flash-back most of the time, to give a little attractant to the fly to get the trout's attention. The leader and tippet start thick and gradually work down in size and diameter, so the flies straighten out perfectly.

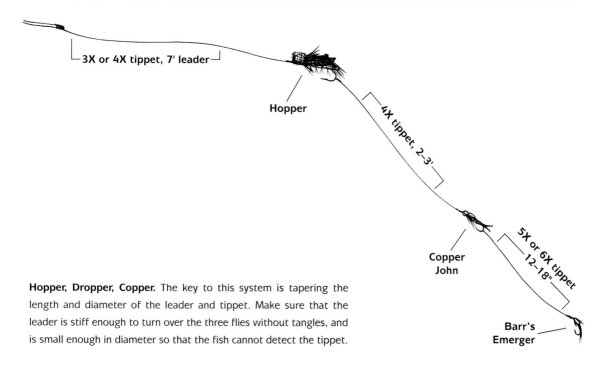

3X or 4X tippet, 7' leader

Hopper

4X tippet, 2-3'

Copper John

5X or 6X tippet 12-18"

Barr's Emerger

Hopper, Dropper, Copper. The key to this system is tapering the length and diameter of the leader and tippet. Make sure that the leader is stiff enough to turn over the three flies without tangles, and is small enough in diameter so that the fish cannot detect the tippet.

The Hopper, Copper, Dropper technique is one of the most effective ways to suspend flies at a consistent water depth during a drift.

John really hit a home run with this simple, unique way of suspending flies that looks natural to the trout. Whether it is a freestone river with a fast deep current or a small tailwater, the Hopper, Copper, Dropper setup is best for wary, suspended, or feeding trout.

Nymphing without an Indicator

You usually get only a few casts to a wary trout before it detects something unnatural and darts away. Larger trout are larger targets for predators, have better eyesight, and larger viewing lanes . . .

Shallow water rigs and presentation

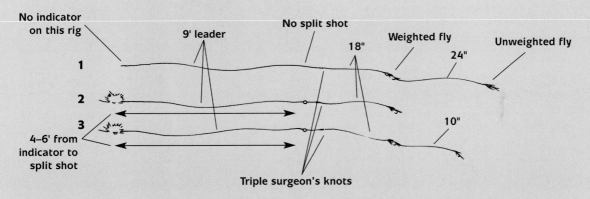

No indicator on this rig   9' leader   No split shot   18"   Weighted fly   24"   Unweighted fly

1

2

3

4–6' from indicator to split shot

10"

Triple surgeon's knots

Three rigging configurations. 1. No split shot, main fly weighted, second fly unweighted: In this rig, look for the splash of the weighted fly. Only one trailing fly reduces the risk of lining the fish. 2. Use a split shot above the surgeon's knot, trailing only one fly eighteen inches below. 3. Split shot with two trailing flies. The first fly is eighteen inches below the split shot, and the second fly is ten inches below the main fly. Rigging two flies close together will decrease the distance from the split shot to the trailing fly, allowing an accurate drift of the imitation short of the trout.

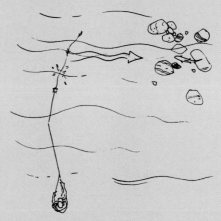

Note that the split shot or weighted fly lands a little short of the fish: a visual key for the angler. The dotted lines show where the flies in the rig pass in front of the fish.

In shallow water it is important to err on the side of caution and cast short of the fish so that you don't snag it.

Midcolumn Rigs and Presentation

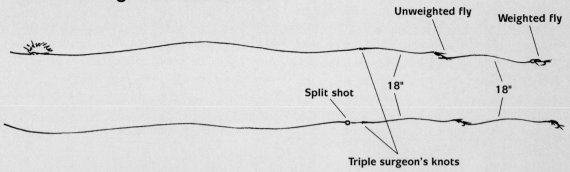

Unweighted fly

Weighted fly

Split shot

18"

18"

Triple surgeon's knots

Two effective leader setups. Use 9' leaders, 4' from indicator to split shot.

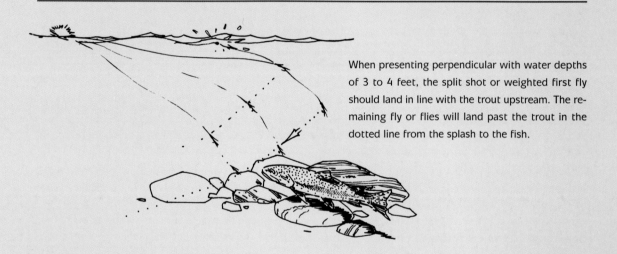

When presenting perpendicular with water depths of 3 to 4 feet, the split shot or weighted first fly should land in line with the trout upstream. The remaining fly or flies will land past the trout in the dotted line from the splash to the fish.

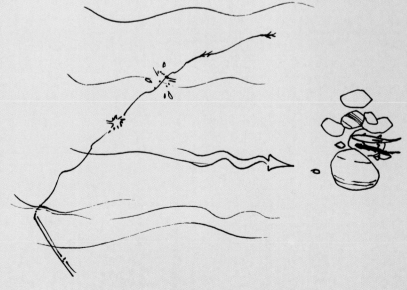

When presenting a fly to a trout in shallow water, always think short. The fly will drift to the side of the trout, giving you opportunities for multiple presentations without the danger of spooking or foul hooking the fish.

not to mention the years of experience that make them doubly spooky. Nymphing without an indicator increases the number of drifts to the trout before it detects you. Even if you only get a few more casts, those few can make all the difference.

I have two ways to rig without strike indicators. One is designed for shallow water and one for deep runs. The adjustment you have to make is to control the sink rate of your flies. A strike indicator or hopper suspends your flies and slows down your sink rate, allowing for a longer drift. Without them, you can compensate by keeping tension on the flies and controlling how fast they dive.

For shallow runs, locate trout holding in water with a good current. The current will move the flies through the run quickly so they won't snag the bottom. In this situation, I put the flies 24 inches apart, and keep the flies as far away from the split shot as possible. The unweighted fly goes last so that it floats higher than the weighted fly. This will give you long drifts and keep the trout from detecting the split shot or seeing the fly touch bottom. Keep tension on the line and leader by not mending, which would cause your flies to sink.

For deep water, use weighted flies to reach the right depth. As with the shallow water setup, keep tension on the fly without allowing it to touch bottom, leading the leader with your rod tip while your flies drift through the run so that there is tension through the rig. Keep the rod tip just above the water's surface, or directly above the flies, so that you can lift and drop the rod tip to attain different depths.

This is similar to the recently popular method of Czech nymphing, except that you can see the trout. Czech nymphing is best for deep, fast water when the trout are on the bottom and not in view. The key to all tight-line methods is to prevent snagging in deep water, while keeping the rig natural and the presentation accurate.

Make sure you know where the flies are in relation to the trout's feeding lane. This is one reason

This char/Dolly Varden was holding in deep water, but I was able to fool it with a tight-line presentation.

so many anglers prefer an indicator: it gives them a sense of where the flies are and where they are traveling. To overcome the lack of indicator, make your lead fly—which can act like an attractor to get the trout's attention—easy to see in the water. This is a common practice in sight-fishing steelhead when the lead fly is an egg; and if you trail another fly below, you see the flies as they drift to the fish, allowing you to force-feed the trout.

Deep Water Rigs and Presentation

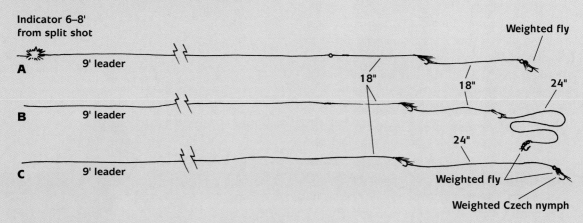

Indicator 6–8'
from split shot

A 9' leader

18"

Weighted fly

18" 24"

B 9' leader

24"

C 9' leader

Weighted fly

Weighted Czech nymph

Three rigs for deep water nymphing. A. Place two flies below a split shot, eighteen inches apart. The trailing fly should be weighted. The flies will sink at the same rate as the split shot. Without weight on the trailing fly, the imitations will drift above the split shot. B. Use three flies. The first two are 18 inches apart, with the trailing fly 24 inches from the second fly. The weighted fly is a heavily weighted fly such as a crane fly larva. C. A two-fly rig with a Czech nymph, tungsten bead, or weighted fly for the dropper. Use this when there is a risk of snagging the bottom. Apply split shot for more depth.

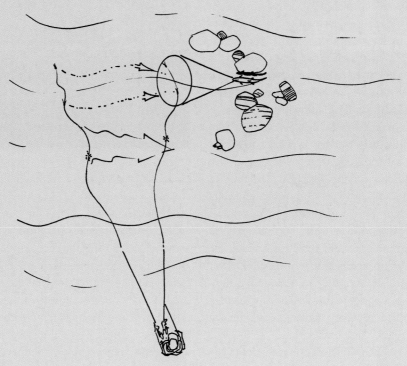

In deep water, cast farther upstream and concentrate on how long it takes for the flies to reach the depth of the trout.

Fly Selection

While there are hundreds of flies on the market today, some are big producers, even after a decade: nymphs like the Pheasant Tail, Hare's Ear, and Copper John, and flies imitating the second stage of the life cycle such as the RS2, Barr's Emerger, and WD40.

Here are some tips. When I am matching the hatch, I try to match the size; however, if I do not have the correct size, I always think small. Insects range in size during the hatch, and trout are more game to take something smaller than the natural rather than a larger imitation. Consider the silhouette of the fly in subsurface conditions. When a fly drops below the water's surface, it darkens; so go darker if your imitation does not match the real thing.

I believe that presentation is more important than fly selection. Trout of all sizes, especially large trout, eat constantly. If a fly looks similar to a food source or looks like an easy meal, a trout will not pass it up.

When you are not matching a hatch or a stage of an active insect, attract trout with an imitation that has a lot of flash, imitates a large food source, or resembles a meal the trout is used to seeing. An example: in the fall when large browns migrate out of a reservoir or large body of water, they are used to feeding on big mayfly *Calibaetis* and midge Chironomid imitations. A large stonefly or midge works well in this situation. Big fish have to eat a lot to survive.

The following flies produce great results on all the waters and with all the trout I encounter. With the number of flies on the market today, and the various hatches on rivers from East to West, it's impossible to list all the effective subsurface flies. Once you have confidence in your presentation, select the flies that regularly produce well. However, don't get stuck in a rut. Many anglers pick a nymph they are comfortable with or have had success with before, and they are unwilling to change.

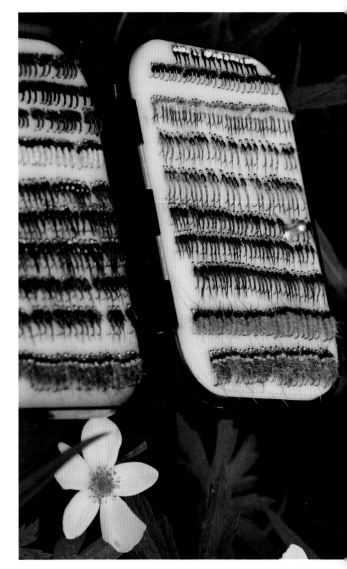

Fish with several sizes of each pattern. Then you can "go small" if the trout are selective.

For instance, in late spring when Blue-Winged Olives are active, a lot of anglers use a Pheasant Tail trailing an RS2, and use the same nymph rig throughout the course of the day. Trout get used to flies quickly, and with all the angling pressure these days, you might do better if you think outside of the box.

Dorsey's Mercury Flashback Pheasant Tail

Mike Mercer's Poxyback Little Yellow Stone

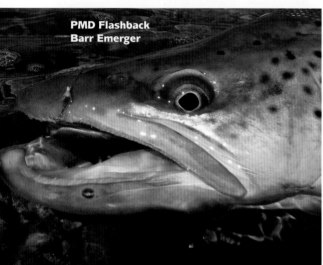

PMD Flashback Barr Emerger

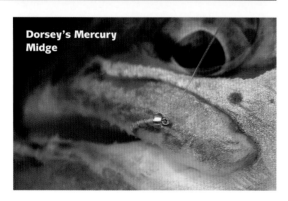

Dorsey's Mercury Midge

Dorsey's Mercury Flashback Pheasant Tail

Hook:	TMC 101 #18-24
Thread:	8/0 Uni-Thread, black
Tail:	Four pheasant tail fibers
Rib:	Copper wire, fine, reverse wrapped
Abdomen:	Four pheasant tail fibers
Wing case:	One strand Pearl Flashabou
Thorax:	Peacock herl
Head:	Black 8/0 Uni-Thread
Bead:	Spirit River glass bead (silver lined), extra small

Mike Mercer's Poxyback Little Yellow Stone

Hook:	TMC 200R #14-16
Thread:	6/0, pale yellow
Tail & antennae:	Pheasant tail fibers
Abdomen:	Pale yellow hare's ear
Rib:	Copper wire
Shellback:	Mottled turkey tail
Wing case:	Mottled turkey tail, epoxied
Thorax:	Pale yellow hare's ear
Legs:	Partridge or grouse
Collar:	Cream hare's ear

PMD Flashback Barr Emerger

Hook:	Wapsi Lighting Strike SE5 #14-20
Thread:	8/0 Uni-Thread, light cahill
Tail:	Brown hackle fibers, clipped
Abdomen:	Wapsi Barr's Emerger dubbing
Thorax:	PMD superfine dubbing
Wing case & legs:	Pale olive hackle fibers
Beadhead:	Optional

Dorsey's Mercury Midge

Hook:	TMC 101 #18-24
Thread:	6/0 Flymaster Plus, white
Rib:	Copper wire, fine, reverse wrapped
Abdomen:	White 6/0 Flymaster Plus
Thorax:	White 6/0 Flymaster Plus
Bead:	Spirit River Mercury Bead, extra small

Garcia's Rojo Midge

Hook:	TMC 200 #16-22
Abdomen:	8/0 black thread
Bead:	Red glass, extra small
Tuft:	Ultra-Floss dental floss
Rib:	Copper Lagartun wire, fine
Collar:	Bright green dyed peacock herl

Garcia's Rojo Midge

Barr's Graphic Caddis

Hook:	TMC 2499 SPBL #14-18
Thread:	8/0 white for abdomen, 8/0 brown for thorax
Tag:	Silver holographic Flashabou
Abdomen:	Micro-tubing, tan or olive
Legs:	Hungarian partridge fibers
Antennae:	Barred lemon wood duck flank fibers
Head:	Natural gray ostrich herl

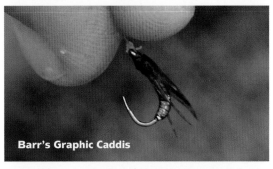

Barr's Graphic Caddis

Barr's Cranefly Larva

Hook:	200R #4-10
Weight:	Lead wire, .035 for a #4
Thread:	6/0 or 70 denier, olive
Tail:	Grizzly marabou
Rib:	3X monofilament
Shellback:	1/4 inch Scudback, Swiss Straw, or Thinskin
Body:	Wapsi Sow-Scud dubbing, olive-gray

Barr's Cranefly Larva

Micro Worm

Hook:	TMC #2457
Thread:	8/0
Body:	Micro chenille, worm brown or red

Micro Worm

Barr's
Tungstone

Barr's Tungstone

Hook:	Teimco 200R #6-10 (dark) and 10-18 (golden), or comparable
Weight:	Lead wire to match hook size
Thread:	8/0 or 6/0, black or brown
Bead:	Tungsten bead sized to fit hook
Tail:	Goose biots, brown or black
Body:	Dubbing color to match pattern: tannish for golden stone, brown or black for dark, and peacock for *Skwala*
Rib:	4X mono
Thorax:	Same type of dubbing as body
Back:	Pearl Flashabou or tinsel under golden stone, or natural Thin Skin
Legs:	Partridge or comparable material

BWO Flashback
Barr Emerger

BWO Flashback Barr Emerger

Hook:	Wapsi lighting Strike SE5 #14-22
Thread:	8/0, iron gray ultra
Tail:	Clipped brown hackle fibers
Abdomen:	Wapsi Barr's Emerger dubbing
Wing case & legs:	Dun hackle fibers
Over wing case:	Mirage opal flash
Beadhead:	optional

Craven's JuJube Midge

Hook:	TMC 2488 #18-24
Thread:	10/0, white
Abdomen:	Super Hair, color combination of your choice, two strands of primary color, one strand of contrasting rib color
Wing case:	White Umpqua Flouro-Fiber
Thorax:	Black tying thread or white thread colored with black marker
Wing buds:	Remaining stubs of Flouro-Fiber from wing case, pulled back along sides of thorax like legs

Craven's
JuJube Midge

Copper John

Hook:	TMC 5262 #10-18
Thread:	70-140 denier, depending on hook size
Bead:	Gold brass or tungsten
Lead:	13 wraps of .010-.020, depending on hook size
Tail:	Brown goose biots
Abdomen:	Copper-colored ultra wire
Thorax:	Peacock herl
Wing case:	Black Thin Skin, with a strand of opal mirage flash pulled over the top, covered with epoxy
Legs:	Mottled brown hen back
Weight:	Gold or tungsten gold bead, and lead wire under thorax

Mayer's Mysis Shrimp

Hook:	TMC 200R #18-14
Thread:	8/0, white
Tail:	White poly yarn
Wing case:	White poly yarn with overlaying pearl Flashabou
Legs:	Clear rubber tentacles, six or seven strands
Abdomen:	White poly yarn under-wrapped with clear midge tubing
Thorax:	White poly yarn
Eyes:	Black rubber eyes

Landon's Larva

Hook:	TMC 200R #20-16
Thread:	8/0, olive
Tail, wing case, & legs:	Pearl Krystal Flash
Abdomen:	Olive goose biot
Thorax:	Gray Ice Dub

Blood Dot

Hook:	Tiemco 2488H #20-14
Thread:	8/0 Uni-Thread, tan
Yoke:	Glo-Bug yarn, egg
Egg:	Glo-Bug yarn, light roe

ANGUS DRUMMOND

JAY NICHOLS

One of my favorite streamers is John Barr's Slump Buster. When this streamer is wet, it has a slim profile with a shiny belly—just like the naturals.

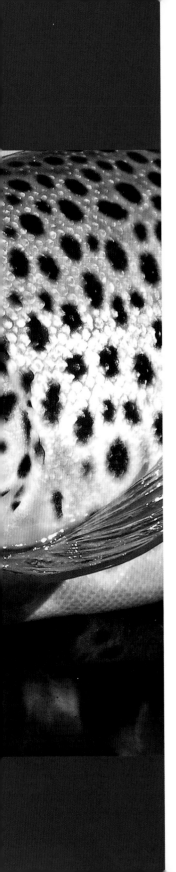

CHAPTER 12

Bugger Time

Streamers are a classic choice when you want to cover a lot of water, but don't overlook sight fishing with streamers. There are the practical reasons: on many streams out West, and on some streams in the East, where the width of the river seems unreasonable for streamers, many anglers just don't fish with them, so you have the opportunity to show the large trout something different than what they usually see. But there are other, less practical, but no less important reasons: watching a trout race over to swipe at the fly is exhilarating.

One significant difference between traditional streamer tactics and sight-fishing streamer tactics is the length of the line that you are casting. Learning how to sight-fish with streamers involves a lot of short casting with floating lines, not just bombing out a lot of line to cover water. You are trying to accurately deliver the fly to the trout.

Tip Preservation Casts

Casting streamers is challenging, and most anglers get into trouble when they try to cast them long distances. Fortunately, in the sight-fishing game, you are generally not casting far. But there are conditions where long casts are necessary. One problem is hitting yourself or your rod tip with these often weighted patterns. Add two flies, which is my favorite setup, and you could go through a few rods if you are not careful. For this reason, I call the next two casts tip preservation casts.

Tip roll cast

The trick to loading your rod at short distances is to keep tension on your line and leader. This allows you to load or flex a fly rod while being able to turn over even the heaviest flies. The tip roll cast lives up to its name in the

151

forward cast. The challenge in fishing streamers is to avoid a lot of false casting, but remain fast in your presentation to the trout.

To begin the cast, take two to three feet of fly line out of the rod tip that is positioned at water level at a downstream angle. The first motion is a Belgian-style, sidearm, upward-angled backcast, stopping at 1 or 2 o'clock. This will allow the rod to gain maximum flex to load, and keep constant tension on the flies to prevent tangles and allow a proper presentation. Once the line is straight behind you, cast forward by rolling the rod tip and releasing the extra line to shoot forward at the beginning of the casting stroke. Stop the rod tip just above the water's surface in the direction your flies will land. The time it takes for your rod tip to reach the water's surface allows the extra line to shoot out.

The trick to gain power from this cast is the wrist roll. I learned this from fellow competitors in casting competitions. Breaking the wrist on the forward cast allows you to shoot 15 to 20 more feet of line: maximum flex and power of the rod in the forward motion of the cast.

Traditionally in the fly-fishing backcasting stroke, you stop your rod at 1 or 2 o'clock with your thumb, wrist, and forearm relatively straight. By bending your wrist on the backcast, your rod tip will stop at 3 o'clock so that it is almost straight behind you. Under normal circumstances, this would be incorrect because the loop is open on the forward cast and the rod tip is convex. But the open loop helps when casting tandem streamers, so the flies do not hit the tip of your rod. In addition, when the rod comes from 3 o'clock and stops at 10 o'clock in front of you on the forward cast, you achieve the maximum flex of your rod, which will cast the streamers effectively.

Open-looped conventional cast

In the traditional casting stroke, your rod tip remains in a straight plane in the forward and backcast to tighten your loops and prevent tailing. But when you throw a lot of weight, you want your flies to stay clear of your rod tip and your body. For this you need to break the conventional mold: have your rod tip travel in a convex path on the forward and backcast stroke. For open loops, stop the rod tip lower on the backcast and forward cast, at 3 and 9 o'clock.

Many anglers watch their backcasts to prevent hitting anything, which can throw you off balance and sometimes cause you to miss the target. The best advice I ever received is to turn around. Make your backcast become the forward casting stroke: you prevent snagging, and you can present and shoot your fly on the backcast. This helps with snags and allows me to be faster and more accurate in my delivery in the worst conditions possible. Wind blowing from the side is one difficult condition: some of the best streamer-fishing conditions are under cloudy, storm-filled, overcast skies, frequently in the wind. If you can switch to a forward or backcast delivery on a moment's notice, you get your flies where they need to go without delay or loss of accuracy.

Presentation

The conventional methods of swinging and fanning water are rewarding. However, when I see trout in a run or in small water with limited casting room, I retrieve the fly so that it approaches the fish head-on, triggering an aggressive reaction.

Whether you are swinging the fly with no movement or aggressively stripping it through a run, there is no wrong way to fish a streamer. If it triggers a strike, you have done your job. The goal is to manipulate streamers to make them look as natural as possible to the trout. Most of the fish you can see are not as willing to attack the fly in clear water where they have less cover. You need to make the streamer look like a swimming baitfish. Sometimes no retrieve at all makes the streamer look like an easy meal—the trout thinks it is a dead-drifting food source. This is an easy meal because it will not

Tip Roll Cast

When you sight-fish with streamers, the trick is to load the rod with the minimum amount of line that you need to achieve the distance. In this sequence, Jay Nichols displays how to load the rod. He uses tension with the tip roll cast and shoots line up to 20 feet with one backcast.

Many people think streamers are just for searching the water, but streamer fishing is an exciting way to sight-fish. When casting streamers, make large loops to prevent tangles or the line hitting your rod. ANGUS DRUMMOND

When retrieving streamers, keep your rod tip low to the water. Tension on the streamer throughout the retrieve allows you to set the hook more efficiently. FRANK MARTIN

have to be chased down. Let the trout tell you what retrieve or presentation it wants.

If the fish does not want to move in the water where it is holding, mix up your retrieves with short and steady pauses. Long, slow retrieves in front of the trout so the fly remains in its view longer can be effective. If that does not work, use multiple short twitches so the fly dances in front of the fish. Changing the movement, not the distance, of the retrieve might be the answer.

If the trout are aggressive, try both long retrieves and short, fast retrieves. I found that the pause is helpful with fast-hitting trout. If you retrieve steadily, the trout will usually attack the food source head on with a swipe. This can lead to missed hits. If you are getting many follows from aggressive and curious trout, a long or short pause can trigger a strike because the trout will see an opportunity to eat.

Upstream Cast and Retrieve

1. Using a single or double haul, cast at an upstream 45-degree angle. Stop the rod tip at the conventional ten o'clock position to shoot the line.

2. When the line lands on the water, begin a large downward mend.   (continued)

3. Continue the large mend by lifting the rod tip a foot or two while moving your body slightly downstream.

4. The mend should stretch from the leader to the rod tip. Drop the rod tip horizontal to the water and continue to rotate your body downstream.

5. When the line is taut at a 45-degree angle, continue moving your body downstream while you begin the retrieve.

6. Still facing downstream, complete your retrieve. This keeps the line tight, allowing every strip to transfer motion to the fly, giving you more control of the retrieve while you watch the flies and the trout.

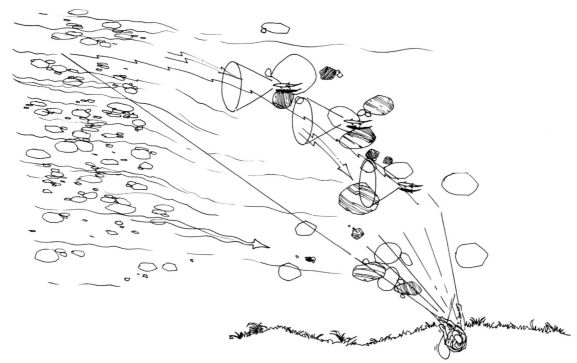

45-degree upstream streamer retrieve. Cast up- and across-stream at a 45-degree angle. Your rig will have time to sink without spooking or lining the trout. Then, with your rod tip at water level, start a retrieve. Keep your line taut as you retrieve the flies. This will allow the maximum number of fish in the run to see your fly.

The up and across presentation

The traditional method for fishing streamers starts with a cast across-stream at the top of the run, letting the fly sink to the trout. Once the fly is deep enough, start a retrieve with the streamer acting like it is escaping away from the fish. While this is an effective way to cover the water in large rivers, it is a problem in tight quarters or tailwaters where you can see the trout. Your presentation is drastically shortened on narrow water, and the fly or flies will line the trout's back if it is high in the run.

To prevent this from happening, cast up- and across-stream at a 45-degree angle, similar to how you start a drift using dry flies or nymphs. Your rig will have time to sink without spooking or lining the trout in the run. Then, with your rod tip at water level, start a retrieve with your body turning downstream toward the bank you are casting on. Keep your line taut as you retrieve your flies through the run. This angle will expose your fly to the maximum number of fish in the run.

With this method, you have a variety of ways to present the fly. If you are fishing in early spring when the trout are lethargic and stage in deep, cold water, a more natural, less aggressive presentation often works. Start by doing slow strips with long pauses, allowing the fly to move and dead-drift in the same retrieve. Or try fast, short strips with short pauses, causing the tail to dance while the eye of the fly lifts and drops like a jig. This is a good retrieve for aggressive trout looking to ambush an injured meal.

The down and across presentation

You can also swing the fly through the run above the trout to give the streamers both movement and the appearance of a dead drift. When the streamer is in front of the fish, twitch the tip of your rod while swinging the fly to make it seem as if the

A 45-degree-angle retrieve shows the fly to more trout in the run. It is a great way to prevent spooking the trout because you present the streamer from downstream.

food source is trying to escape. If you do this at an exaggerated angle upstream of the trout in a low-tuck body position, you won't spook the trout and you will get more hookups.

Trout in shallow riffles or runs prefer to stay stationary because there is no room for them to move up or down as they would in deep water. Their viewing lanes are incredibly narrow, and if the fly is not presented a foot or two in front of

Below: **Presenting streamers downstream.** Position yourself far enough upstream that your streamer can swing without rubbing the body or snagging the fish. Start your retrieve a few seconds after your flies land. Many of your strikes will be at the end of the presentation as the streamers move upstream, resembling escaping prey.

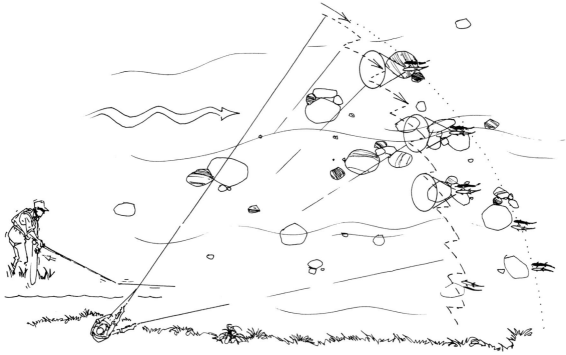

When dead-drifting streamers, twitch the fly without stripping it out of the lane that it is drifting in. The streamer pulsates and wiggles like a wounded baitfish, and a trout can't pass up an easy meal.

During high water, trout can find cover even under bluebird skies and will eat without being wary. Jay Nichols fooled this aggressive male rainbow with streamers on a warm summer day.

them, they will not see it. This is why a drift to a swing at the end will target that specific trout, and maybe even entice others in the area to attack. Remember that the key to the swing is to leave enough space above the trout so that your fly or leader will not rub the fish, spook it, or snag it.

The dead drift

Trout, especially large trout, are lazy by nature, but they will not pass up protein-rich food if they can get it without expending energy. Take, for example, the world-record browns that hold in the Ozark fisheries. A huge part of their diet is the dead shad that drift downstream from the turbulent dams and the thousands of rainbows that are dumped into the deep runs where these giants wait. Drifting a streamer imitates these easy meals.

To be most effective with this presentation, select a section of fast water. Turbulent water causes the loose materials on the streamer to pulsate and look like an easy, injured meal. Dead-drifting after casting across-stream, or at an upward angle, produces results. If the water is shallow, simply follow the fly line with the tip of your rod. If the water is deep, apply a mend or two to keep your streamer deep.

The fly can drift drag-free, but you can still impart subtle motion to attract trout. As you dead-drift the fly through a run, keep the fly line in your left hand next to the reel and cork handle. While the fly is drifting in the run, pull in and release around six inches of line as the streamer moves. Don't let go of the line. This give-and-take method during the streamer drift wiggles your fly and entices fish.

Streamer Water

Many fish that are candidates for a streamer are hiding and you can't see them. Think about where the trout has cover and can ambush a meal. Cover

Shallow riffles are overlooked streamer spots—most anglers target deep runs and pools.

can be structure, but cover is also deep water or turbulent runs. I always look first to the deep water where there might be quality aggressive trout.

Deep water

Trout are less wary in high flows and stained water, making this one of my favorite streamer times. The amount of food during these increased flows can be incredible. But finding where the fish are holding is difficult in high water because the fish can spread out so much. Searching for a fish with a streamer will reveal some new hiding grounds.

Don't ignore deep water around drop-offs, deep runs, or deep, slow moving, stagnant waters. And don't forget the water between the deep runs: these areas can hold quality fish as well. Pocketwater around structure, deep eddies on the edge of a run, and (one of my favorite areas) impressions on the river bottom in shallow water are all places where trout can hold, hidden from predators.

You can't see fish as well in deep water. Look for silhouettes or shadows and present to those targets. In these conditions, when the trout has taken the streamer, you'll either see the fish move or you'll see the white of the fish's mouth.

Shallow water

Some of the best streamer fishing is in shallow water where it is easier to see the trout and its behavior. When fish feed in shallow water, they have only a few seconds to react before committing to a food source. The viewing lane is narrow, allowing only a short glance at potential meals. Also, when something like a streamer is stripped through the water in front of them, they become territorial and react by attacking or swiping at a fly.

In shallow water, adjust the weight of your flies and how fast you retrieve them so that you do not snag the bottom. I keep tension on the streamer throughout the retrieve and drift, helping it ride high in the water column. A good retrieve speed shortens the time the trout has to investigate my imitation. Many anglers pass up this water, thinking it is not deep enough or suitable for streamers, but if you apply tension with a constant retrieve, you will not snag the bottom and you will fool more trout.

A loop knot lets the fly wiggle back and forth on the retrieve. This erratic action, whether with an active or dead-drift retrieve, entices trout because the fly appears to be injured.

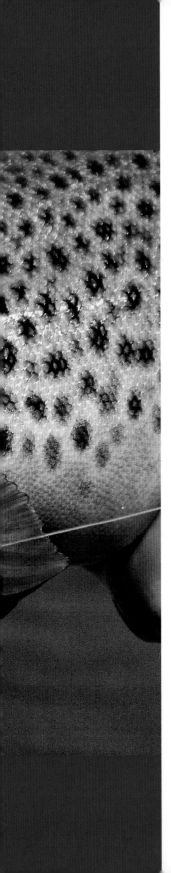

CHAPTER 13

Rigging Streamers

Design your setup to get the fly or flies to the depth where the trout are holding. Use sinking lines, sink-tip lines, or weighted streamers on a floating line. Rigging correctly with different setups gives all trout in the run a chance to see the fly.

Selecting the Right Line

I know there are gearheads who like to buy extra spools for their reels (and lug them around), but when you are hunting trout, less is more. When I fish streamers, I use a floating line 90 percent of the time. It prevents snags on the river bottom and gives a more natural presentation in shallow and narrow waterways. Instead of relying on the line to sink your flies to the trout's holding depth, a weighted streamer with lead wrap or a tungsten cone gets the job done.

My favorite line for streamers is the Clouser line from RIO. With a heavy front taper, the line is able to turn over large flies and heavy rigs with ease. In addition to using the correct line, consider up-lining by one weight, which flexes your rod more deeply on shorter casts and allows you to load it more efficiently. You can use a sinking leader or a weighted fly to get down deep enough.

One difficulty when retrieving weighted or unweighted streamers on a floating line is that the flies travel toward the tip of the fly line on the surface of the water. The streamer travels at an upward angle toward the rod tip. This movement might seem unnatural to trout because any small baitfish or insect is not going to travel to the surface where many predators lurk waiting for a meal. They would rather stay low and below the surface for

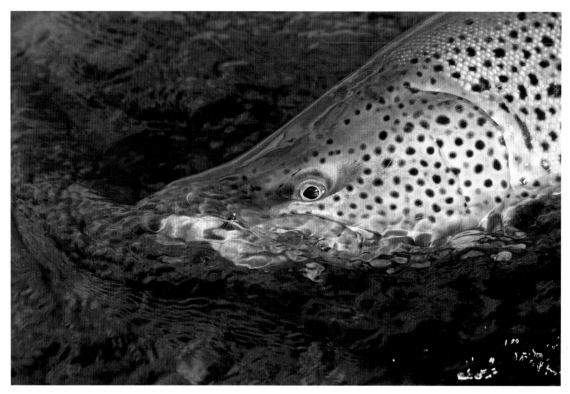

This quality brown was holding at the bottom of a deep seam run that would have been impossible to reach without a sink-tip line.

some protection. Sink-tip lines are effective in these sight-fishing situations.

Sight fishing means fishing waters of different depths. I use a sink-tip line when I need my streamer to get down to the depth of the trout in deep runs and drop-offs. The huge advantage to this is that the streamer stays at the same depth, in view of all the trout below. It is effective in shallow water if the current is fast enough to push the line through without snagging. Or you can compensate with a very fast retrieve.

Check the sink ratio of the line you are purchasing (usually gauged by inches per second) to make

sure the grain of the sink-tip will work for your waters. If you need to use a sink-tip or sinking line, try to get one with interchangeable heads that you can change quickly out on the water.

When you are fishing streamers, trout see the fly first, so there is no need to fish with tippets less than 0X or 1X.

A full-sink line is a versatile tool to use while fishing for trout, steelhead, and salmon worldwide. The advantage to a full-sink line is the constant depth you get during the retrieve. The fly is constantly sinking as you step it back. This is an effective way to fish large, deep rivers, and it is extremely effective on reservoirs where there are big drop-offs. While it is effective, choose the water where you fish full-sink wisely. If you don't, the presentation will be altered, and the bottom will become your enemy as you snag it all day long.

I guided for a year in Alaska where I became very familiar with sink-tips. We fished big, deep rivers for trout and salmon where the only way to reach the deep-dwelling migratory fish was with a sink-tip. Sight fishing with such a deep presentation depends on locating the fish and casting to where they are holding.

There are many ways to get a visual of the trout. If you can get a visual, no matter what the circumstance, then you are sight fishing, even if the fish are not visible from the river's edge.

On fly-out trips in Alaska, the pilot would fly overhead and turn the plane to give an aerial view of the fish and where they were holding. This look from above is great for anglers targeting Atlantic salmon, whether it is from a plane or staring down from a high bank into 20 or 30 feet of clear water. In these deep-water conditions, a sink-tip line gets you down to where you can show your retrieve to deep-dwelling monsters!

Leader and Tippet Selection

While fishing streamers you can use heavy leaders and tippets that prevent the trout from breaking off before the knot pulls loose. I got this advice from my good friend John Barr. I was using 3X for streamers, but John said, "If the fish is willing to commit to taking a streamer on 3X fluorocarbon, it will not shy away from a streamer on 0X fluorocarbon. This will stop break-offs and let you land a majority of the trout you hook." Boy, was he right!

Using heavier tippets and leaders, the knots can fail before the material does, so it is critical to tie strong knots.

I now use nothing but 0X leaders and tippets for streamers, and I hook and land more fish.

If you are fishing a sink-tip line, use a shorter leader so that the fly stays close to the river bottom. For floating lines, use a longer leader to so that the flies can sink to where the trout are holding. I prefer to use a longer leader when fishing streamers, whether I have a sinking or floating line, so that the trout have less chance of detecting my fly line. For sinking lines, I use 7- or 8-foot leaders, and for floating lines, 8- to 11-foot leaders. I have more versatility and can place the fly or flies above the trout without spooking the target.

Knots

The first step in rigging for streamers starts with a powerful knot, capable of holding without pulling loose. Light tippet material will break before the knot pulls loose. In streamer situations, you want material that is so strong that the first thing to give will be the knot. A correctly-tied knot can keep the trout you have on until the fish is in the net.

Notice the rust Slump Buster in the corner of this rainbow's jaw. In my opinion, this fly is one of the best imitations of a baitfish on the market today. ROSS PURNELL

When I first started fly fishing, I learned the clinch knot for tying on dry flies and nymphs with light tippets, ranging from 4X to 6X. I learned that this knot has less bulk on the eye of the hook, and is strong enough to hold the trout. Flies look more natural as they drift downstream. This has worked well on light tippets, but leads to disaster using heavy materials. The knot pulls loose with heavy tippets and leaders because the material cannot cinch properly. The solution is the improved clinch knot; it is easy to tie and can mean the difference between landing a trophy trout or watching the fish get away.

The non-slip loop knot allows the streamer to dance up, down, and side-to-side while it drifts or is stripped through a run. This can be incredibly helpful when you are trying to provoke a trout to hit your fly.

Fly Selection

With the many variations of streamers and buggers on the market today, narrowing down your selection can be difficult. Large, unconventional-looking streamers are more effective when trout are making predatory attacks on the flies. In situations when the trout are eating injured baitfish or relying on a food source like small fry or escaping crayfish, a more realistic size and slim-bodied look is best. Have a selection of both so that you are prepared. This is especially helpful in clear water when you see the trout to which you are presenting the fly. The fish will not move far to take the streamer in clear water, and when there are bluebird skies with no security from above, the fish prefer to wait for injured prey to drift into their feeding lanes.

Picking the correct streamer imitation starts with reading the trout's behavior. If trout are aggressive, attractor patterns are ideal. When fish are selective, a natural imitation with a slim profile is best. Try different flies and read the behavior of the fish.

I always simplify my fly selection based on what food source is in the water. For example, if there are a lot of brown-trout fry in the river, I choose a rust or tan pattern. This natural imitation is ideal in steady, slow, clear water because the trout are looking for the natural food sources.

If flows increase the day before you head up to the river, it will stain the water and deepen areas that were shallow. Your ability to see the fish will be compromised, and so is the trout's ability to see you. These conditions warrant a change to brighter, more attractive streamers with flash to get the trout's attention.

There are two basic types of streamers: attractors with flashy materials intended to get the trout's attention, and natural imitations resembling the slim profile of a baitfish, sculpin, or other prey. These attractor patterns are effective when fish are preparing to spawn and are aggressively guarding water, or in deep, warm water when the trout are more active and can move without the threat of predators from above. This is some of the most exiting sight fishing: when you watch a trout race off to annihilate a large, bright streamer in clear water, it makes the hair on the back of your neck stand up.

I prefer high water, prespawn timing, and warm conditions when I sight-fish with attractor streamers. These are the best times to get aggressive takes because the trout are more active in these condi-

This brown was willing to eat a chartreuse and white Clouser Minnow in extremely low flows. The natural look of the fly in the water fools even the wariest trout. No matter where you travel, this is a good pattern to have in your box.

Attractor imitations work for sight fishing other fish as well. This char/Dolly Varden chased down a black and blue Meat Whistle from twenty feet away.

tions than at any other time of year. You immediately know if the trout are looking for a big meal after the first cast and retrieve. If you don't get even a look from the fish you have spotted, consider using a more natural imitation.

To select the right attractor, determine the main food supply in the water. For example, if you are fishing a large river in Montana with a large abun-

A baby brown and a fly that does a good job of imitating it. To select a quality streamer that looks natural to the trout, get it wet to see how the fly and profile look in the water.

dance of sculpin, your fly should imitate the natural food source—something like Mike Lawson's Conehead Sculpin with the addition of flash, sili legs, or materials added to attract the fish. On the other hand, if you are fishing fair-sized tailwaters with a huge supply of crayfish, imitate and match the color of the natural food source (while adding attracting materials to it), like John Barr's Meat Whistle.

When the trout are less aggressive, lethargic, or are holding in shallow water with less cover, use a streamer with less flash that imitates a natural food source. The trout may not move far when they are

lethargic. The less movement the trout makes, the better its chances for survival are. With a more natural-looking fly and a slower retrieve, the trout can consume the meal without expending too much energy.

I use more natural-looking flies in winter, early spring, late fall, in clear or shallow water, and for any wary fish. If you do decide to go with the realistic fly, be sure to allow long pauses with every retrieve so that the trout, if it chooses to follow the fly, has a chance to eat it as it drifts.

Profile is important when selecting streamers. The Woolly Bugger, which is a great fly used

Improved
clinch knot

—— 18" ——

Non-slip
mono loop knot

Double slump rig. Fishing two streamers allows you to get deep into the river, to trout you cannot see. Use tungsten cones, lead eyes, or lead wrap on two flies to increase the weight of your rig. If there is too much weight, adjust by using an unweighted fly.

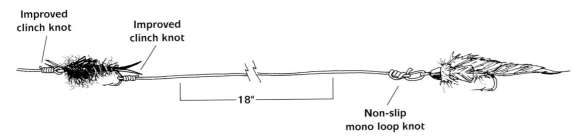

Never leave for the river in the spring or fall without a chasing-baitfish rig. Trout go crazy when you use an apricot 6mm egg.

worldwide for many different species of fish, elicits a reaction-based strike. When you stop the fly in the water, the hackle fibers stick out to the side; during the pause, it gets a fish's attention. However, this can also have the opposite effect on trout you can see, and in cooler water where trout are less active, because the fly does not look like a baitfish. That is when you need a slim-profile fly, which allows you to do more in the retrieve by manipulating the fly. A slim body and profile is why many successful flies, like the Slump Busters and Clouser Minnows, don't stay in the fly bins. They work in some of the world's most pressured waters.

Double Streamers

When you are sight fishing with streamers, you can add a second fly to give the fish more options of color, size, and shape. I refer to these two-fly setups as double-trouble rigs.

My favorite double streamer setup is the "double slumps." I use different colors and sizes of John Barr's streamer, the Slump Buster: the lead fly is a #4; and eighteen inches below that, the trailing fly

is a #6. I keep the sizes the same and change the colors—my golden ticket for rivers all over the United States.

You can mix an attractor and a natural imitation. I keep my lead fly a natural imitation with a slightly brighter appeal. My favorite fly for this is Mike Lawson's Conehead Wool Sculpin in tan. It's a great fly to use when you want to see the fly as you are stripping it through the water or drifting it to the trout. From the back of the sculpin, trail something bright, big, and ugly—like a Krystal-bodied egg-sucking leech. That way you will know if the trout is more likely to take an attractor streamer or the natural imitation, located eighteen inches above.

If you really want to get the trout's attention, put a food source imitation above the streamer to make it look like a small fry chasing a meal. I think trout look at this as competition, and a double food source triggers strikes. To determine what fly to place above the streamer, match it to the food supply that is prevalent in the water. For example, in the summer, the browns consider stoneflies in the water an easy meal.

The best way to tire a trout is to make it shake its head and thrust its whole body side to side. Mark Gebauer holds the rod correctly on a violently head-shaking giant brown.

CHAPTER 14

Seeing the Fight

Sight fishing goes beyond spotting, stalking, and presenting your flies to fish you can see. Seeing the trout and its movements throughout the fight increases your chances of landing the fish, preparing you for the moves you need to make throughout the battle. This chapter will help you understand how to avoid the breaking point in a fight, while maintaining maximum pressure on the trout, resulting in a quick landing.

Know Your Battleground

The best chance a trout has to break off during a fight is to escape to waters filled with obstacles, like structure or fast current. Even before you cast, know the water above and below the spot you're fishing and map out a strategy on how to get the trout in the net.

Look for obstacles (structure) in the water that the trout might use to escape once it feels the pressure you apply to its mouth. Imagine how the fish will try to relieve the pressure it feels from the fly. This is normally a series of head shakes, combined with a number of runs up- or downstream. With a game plan for fighting the fish, you can concentrate more on the trout and its movements during the fight instead of the water it is heading for. If there are rocks in the middle of the run, be prepared to get as close to them as possible and use your rod tip to guide the trout out of the troubled area. When the fish is in a fast current, bring your rod to the side to get the trout out of water that will increase the pressure on the tippet. These are all situations you can see coming before the fight by studying the water.

Correct rod position and calculated pressure can make for a quick fight.

Setting the Hook

Think about where you want your fly when you set the hook. The corner of the mouth keeps the fly out of the teeth-filled upper and lower jaws, and gives you a chance to lift the trout's head to get it into the net quickly. To set in the corner of the mouth, try to set the hook at a downstream angle.

Water depth and your position relative to the fish are two important factors to consider when setting the hook. Water depths—whether shallow or deep—play a role in the trout's reaction and how you adjust to it. In shallow water, your hook set should be fast, and you should keep the rod tip relatively low. The fish's first reaction is violent head shaking. If the trout cannot retreat to deep water, it

A downstream hook set ensures that the fly ends up in the corner of the trout's mouth, which will prevent the fly from coming loose later in the fight. ANGUS DRUMMOND

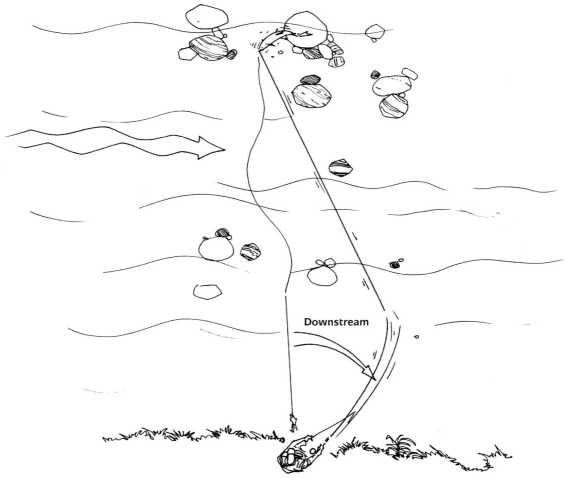

Downstream

Setting the hook on an across-stream set. To place the fly in the corner of the trout's mouth, the trick is to not break the imaginary line that runs in the plane of your shoulder. If the rod tip passes this plane, the graphite cannot flex any more, and the pressure goes to the tippet, resulting in a break-off. If you stop at the right time and place—before the shoulder plane—you will have time to bring the rod to a safe shock-absorbing position in front of your body.

will run quickly after the explosion of head shaking. This makes it risky to keep the rod high where it cannot flex any more to absorb the power from the run. This causes many fish to break off.

Instead, keep the rod horizontal with a slight bend; let the reel absorb the violent run until the trout turns upstream or finds deeper water. Then return the rod to a vertical position. This adjustment ensures that you keep pressure on the trout without overdoing it and losing the fish.

This is incredibly helpful when you are fishing dry flies and the trout is above the surface. When it takes the fly and begins to shake its head, the run will be lightning fast.

Water depth

In deep water, the trout has the advantage of time; it shakes its head on the way to the surface to dislodge the fly, and it goes deep to find cover as it turns up or downstream. Imagine a line going

John Barr displays how to drop the rod to a slightly horizontal position while a wild Colorado rainbow bolts downstream. In this position, your reel applies the correct pressure with the drag.

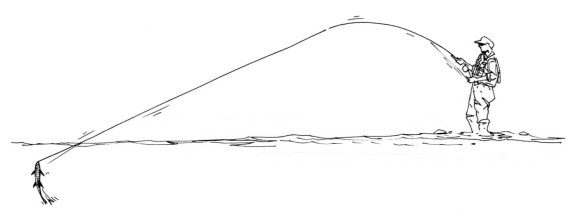

Lifting a fish. One of the most effective ways to maintain maximum pressure during the fight is to lift from a horizontal position. Reel down to the trout and keep your elbow at the side of your body. Lift while keeping the rod horizontal. This applies power from the strongest point of the rod, the butt section.

The reel is one of the most important tools for fighting trout. It allows you to retrieve without over-applying power. Large trout can break even 4X tippet with one powerful head shake.

straight downstream from the plane of your shoulder. When you lift the rod at an upward angle downstream after the trout eats, you don't want to break the plane of your shoulder with the rod behind you. If you do, the rod will reach its maximum flex and apply all the pressure to your tippet, resulting in more break-offs. To adjust, when you see a fish head-shaking to the surface after you set, allow the trout to pull your arm down slightly with each aggressive body movement, but keep your arm and rod in front of this imaginary line. This will prevent you from pulling up too hard, causing your leader or tippet to reach its breaking point.

This deep-water movement can be some of the most powerful thrusts in a fight, especially in fast water. Even if you can see the fish's reaction, you will know when it has started or stopped these violent body movements, and you can drop your arm while still maintaining a bend. Think of your arm as a shock absorber for the rod, or an extension similar to the flex you would get from a Spey rod.

Imagine hooking a weighted object in a deep run and bringing the object to the surface without breaking the leader and tippet. This is a great way to approach every deep-water fight. If you keep your rod at a slightly horizontal position, and prevent over-flexing the rod, you can wait patiently as the trout shakes its head to the water's surface before it dives or runs again.

Riverside position

When you see the trout from different river positions, you increase your chances of landing it. Most fish are lost in the first fifteen seconds or the last fifteen seconds of the fight. Many anglers forget to adjust their position when they focus on the water where they see the trout. Each position—above, across-stream, or below—requires a specific rod position to set the hook.

When you are above the fish, the challenge is to lift and put pressure on the trout without pulling the fly out of its mouth. Any vertical lift

One of the biggest challenges for any angler is guiding trout around structure while remaining in control of the fight.
ANGUS DRUMMOND

from the rod pulls the fly away from the trout's jaw. You must be patient when the trout takes the fly, and make sure when you see the fish eat, that it has come back down on the fly (when fishing dry flies) or that it has closed its mouth on the fly (in subsurface conditions). Once you see the take, lift your arm, keeping the rod vertical to the trout with a slight bend in the rod. The tension and power from the trout are on your reel—without applying too much power, allowing the trout to break off.

This rod position buys you time to quickly run or move downstream to get perpendicular to the trout. When you are downstream of (or perpendicular to) the fish, bring your rod to a vertical position. This keeps the trout from breaking off and allows the reel to do its job without pulling the fly out of the trout's mouth.

The best position to set the hook is across from or slightly downstream of the trout, as illustrated on page 173. From these positions, you can control where the fly is in the trout's mouth and hold the rod at the right angle when you set. Many anglers become too comfortable lifting vertically—which can work, but sometimes it just barely penetrates the top of the trout's mouth and the fly comes loose later in the fight. One thing is for sure: never set upstream from this position. You will pull the flies away from the trout, or just barely nick the fish's mouth.

To perform the set correctly: After the trout takes your fly, lift the rod at a 45-degree downstream angle or sideways, with the rod tip a foot or so above the water. Don't allow the rod tip to break the plane of your shoulder. Once the tip has broken the imaginary line from your shoulder downstream, the rod has reached its maximum flex, allowing the trout to break off. When the trout begins to shake its head, bring your rod back to a vertical position. The fly will be in the corner of the trout's jaw, the best place to apply maximum pressure and control during the rest of the fight.

If you are below the trout, your hook set is a little bit more forgiving. The main objective is to elevate the rod to place the fly correctly. Remember that your main goal after the set is to gain control: get to the river's edge and move upstream to prevent the fish from swimming upstream and finding structure, or bolting downstream at you, causing the line to go slack.

Keep your rod pointed at 11 o'clock throughout the lift, and raise your arm as you lift the rod. This keeps your rod high enough to get the proper tension on your line: your arm adds more length. By keeping the rod at 11 o'clock, you can drop the rod tip to adjust to a run when the trout begins to fight. To maximize the hook set, make sure that you wait until the trout closes its mouth on the fly before you lift.

Adjusting Position

The first adjustment you need to make during the fight is your position, whether in the water or on the bank. Move in response to the trout's reactions: that keeps you in control and allows you to land trout quickly, especially larger fish. The biggest mistake you can make is to remain stationary while the fish is in motion.

Stay as close to the action as possible throughout the fight; this lets you see the fish better and gives you the chance to move and adjust based on the trout's movements. Maintain maximum pressure for fewer break-offs.

When you fight the trout, try to stay perpendicular or slightly downstream of the fish. While doing so, keep your rod vertical to maintain maximum pressure during the fight. I refer to this as "walking the dog": you are keeping the trout on a short leash as you travel upstream and downstream with the fish.

You need to know how to react to the trout's behavior while you play the game of follow-the-leader. For instance, at the beginning of a fight, if a trout bolts upstream, get to an area where you can move quickly, either on the bank or in shallow water. As you follow the trout, remain a few steps downstream of the fish. This gives you a head start when the fish turns to move back downstream. Watch the trout while periodically glancing at the ground to make sure you stay upright. You will be in charge of the fight, prepared to react to what is ahead.

If the trout bolts downstream, try to remain a few steps in front of it until it turns to face upstream or stops to shake its head. A fish moving downstream will move faster than it would in stillwater. If the run is too much and you simply cannot keep up, place your rod tip downstream in line with you while maintaining a bend. This maintains pressure to the side of the trout's jaw as if you were still applying pressure while standing perpendicular to the trout.

Seeing the Head Shake

One the greatest feelings during any fight is the powerful thrust you feel all the way to your shoulder as the fish shakes its head to dislodge the fly. Some of these are so powerful that the head of the trout will almost touch its tail as it moves side to side.

The fastest way to end a fight with any trout is to make it shake its head. The violent motion of the fish thrusting its body side-to-side tires the trout faster than when it runs. The largest trout I have seen are landed in less than seven minutes using this technique. However, this is also how many anglers lose the fight because these violent motions can stress your rig to the breaking point. To prevent this from happening to you, allow your arm to be pulled down for each powerful thrust. If you are a good distance away from the trout, point the rod at the fish and let your drag do all the work from your reel.

There are particular dilemmas to overcome with two-fly rigs when the trout start to head shake. The first is that the lead or trailing fly will snag the trout's body as it tumbles about in the water, causing a break off. The second is that the tippet and leader might wrap around the trout's body like a tetherball, taking the pressure off the fly and causing it to dislodge.

To prevent either of these dilemmas, adjust the placement of your rod when the fish starts head-shaking. When you apply pressure to the trout, your rod should be directly above the trout or slightly downstream at a 45-degree angle. This po-

Be sure to return the rod to the vertical position as soon as the head shaking stops to prevent the trout from regaining balance. ANGUS DRUMMOND

sition will trigger the fish to move sideways, shaking its head. When the trout starts to shake its head, move the rod tip upstream while the fish spins, rolls, and head shakes to relieve the pressure. This will keep the trout from wrapping up in the rig or snagging the second fly. When the fish begins to run or stops head shaking, return the rod to the vertical position or downstream.

Adjusting the Rod

When you move your rod in reaction to the trout's movements, you maintain control during the fight, regardless of structure in the water, different current speeds, and the trout's struggles.

First of all, every time the trout violently shakes its head, drop the rod slightly from the vertical position. The key is to maintain a bend during this movement to prevent any slack in your line that could cause the fly to dislodge from the trout's mouth.

Second, when the trout makes a bolting run, instead of keeping your rod vertical (running the risk of reaching its maximum flex and causing the tippet or leader to break), drop your rod to a horizontal position and point the rod tip at the trout. This will apply all the force to the reel, allowing the ball-bearing disc drag to compensate for the power. When the trout has stopped running, return the rod back to a vertical position. This will help you learn the breaking point and keep you from applying too much pressure to your rod.

For rivers or sections of water where there is no structure, these techniques are all you have to worry about; but as we all know, an obstacle-free river is rare. In most rivers, it is a struggle to keep a quality trout from breaking off on the obstacles in the river. In fast water, the trout has the upper hand: it can gain control early in the fight using its speed and the fast-moving water. One trick to use at the beginning of the fight, or thereafter when the trout comes to the surface to head shake, is to

When you are around structure the more line you have out, the less control you have. Stay as close to the trout as possible and keep your rod high. Use the rod tip to guide the trout around the structure in the river.

apply sideways maximum pressure: while the fish is off-balance and disoriented, guide it into slower, shallow water along the river's edge. Then you can gain line and stay in control with the vertical position of your rod.

Keep a close eye on the trout when you fight it around structure. If you are in close quarters, place the rod directly above the trout. If you have distance between you and the fish, then keep the rod tip pointed at the trout in a high, vertical position. When you are close to the trout, keep the rod in a horizontal position, maintaining a bend, and guide the rod tip around the structure in line with the trout. This will keep the trout from fraying the leader and breaking off. When the opportunity presents itself, place your rod sideways to steer it away from the structure.

If there is a considerable distance between you and a fish that bolts around something in the river, keep the rod tip at a high vertical position in line with the trout, hoping that the line will remain above the structure when the fish is on the run. If you are stuck on the structure, then point the rod at the structure with the rod completely straight. That allows the pressure to be applied to the reel. Strip out a fair amount of excess line. Once you think you have the right amount of line out to match the distance between you and the structure, pinch the line briefly and perform a roll cast over the structure in a last-ditch effort to free the line. I've tried this "Hail Mary" in encounters with large trout, and it helps land the trophy. For fast or turbulent water, use sideways leverage to pull the trout from the line-ripping current.

Adjusting for the Run

Managing line when a trout runs is tricky. The best thing to do is to clear the line while maintaining a bend, never releasing the pressure applied to the trout. Notice how John Barr keeps the line clear of his body and reels when the trout bolts upstream, allowing the reel to apply the pressure.

When the trout is at the surface of the water headshaking and off balance, you can net the fish without worrying about the last-minute bolt.

The prize comes to hand.

Notice that when Angus Drummond goes in with his net to scoop this big 'bow, the trout's mouth is out of the water, preventing it from swimming away.

Sight-Fishing Techniques to Apply Pressure

The key to fighting fish, especially large fish, is to apply the maximum pressure your tippet can stand—and no more. Too much pressure can lead to a lost fish. You need to apply maximum pressure to control the fish and the land it quickly.

Anglers often try to apply pressure to the trout by using the tip of the rod. While this sometimes works, you run the risk of fighting the trout to the point of exhaustion, which can kill it after you release it. And the fish has a better chance of spitting the fly out because of the lack of tension. I think that some anglers are not familiar with the breaking point, and they do not want to lose the trout.

To overcome this fear, and to successfully apply maximum pressure without breaking off, you must understand how to lift up on the trout while adjusting to any sudden power applied by the fish. Do this by using the butt section of the rod: it is the strongest section, designed to apply maximum power. Keep the rod pointed up from a horizontal position or a 45-degree angle. Then with the rod tip low, lift up on the rod while extending your arm. This lifts the trout's head, making it shake its head instead of powering down toward the river bottom.

Your arm will get tired as the fight drags on. When it does, put the reel seat against your forearm, or put the bottom of the rod against your chest or stomach. Just be sure the reel is not obstructed and can turn freely.

The best way to determine if you need to apply pressure is to watch the trout. If the fish is powering down or holding in a particular area in the river, you need more lift from your rod. You know you have the advantage if it keeps moving during the whole course of the fight. Always remember that the faster you land a trout correctly, the better its chances to live and fight another day.

Seeing Gains

One of the most important pieces of equipment is a quality reel. Some anglers prefer to get the fish on the reel, while others prefer to strip in line to control the trout. My opinion is that it is best to get the fish on the reel so that the drag will properly release the line. Then when you need to gain line, do so by reading the trout's movements during the fight. This will let you gain line constantly and keep the trout on a short leash.

To gain line effectively, reel down to the fish or the water's surface. This is simple to do when your rod is at a 45-degree angle most of the time, not straight up in the air. When the trout pauses at any time during fight, even if only for a few seconds, gain line by reeling quickly, with your rod slowly moving down to a vertical position while maintaining a bend to apply pressure. This

won't give the fish any breathing room, so it will tire quickly.

When you are reeling in line, make sure your motions are quick, and always anticipate another run. I teach others to do two or four quick turns of the reel, and then let go. If you repeat this process throughout the fight, you don't have to worry about your hand being in the way if the fish runs. Once you learn this quick reel technique, you will be in control of your line and the trout on it.

Knowing When to Net

This is one of the best parts of the fight—when you can see the trout. Every move you make when it comes to netting the fish is based on its movements in the water. You do not have to fight a trout to the point of exhaustion. Instead, rely on the trout to lose its balance when it shakes its head at the surface. My favorite situation is when the trout rolls on the surface of the water and has to reposition for a second when it gets upright from this unusual position.

Remember, almost all trout will give a last burst of effort when you first try to net them; this is why netting the trout head first is mandatory. When the trout rolls and head shakes on the surface for longer periods at the end of the fight—that is your moment. Use your arm as an extension, point it up and back behind you at a 45-degree angle, and then extend your netting hand out as far as you can to scoop up the unbalanced trout. This will help you gain control during those last heart-pounding fifteen seconds of the fight.

There is so much more to a fight on the water when you are sight fishing than just lifting your rod and hoping for the best. You must be in control, and on top of every movement the trout can make. The techniques and adjustments you just learned will help you anticipate the trout's fighting ways but, more important, they will allow you to land fish quickly, ensuring the trout's safety.

Once you or your partner has spotted a trout, make sure you both see it. The casting angler then gets into the best position for good presentation with the other angler's guidance.

CHAPTER 15

The Buddy System

The buddy system is the collaboration of two anglers working together to sight-fish; one angler is the spotter while the other angler is the caster. It all starts with communication between two anglers on the water, resulting in more trout on the line. Many encounters with trout require two pair of eyes to get the job done.

Sight fishing as a team takes practice and coordination, which is built over time on the water together. When you fish with someone long enough, you learn their ways, and this collaboration of four eyes is always better than two. Instead of getting to the river and breaking away from your companion, use the knowledge and techniques of your buddy to catch more fish—or at least to catch that one trophy. You both will have the satisfaction of knowing you got the job done as a team.

Communication

Many places on the river have only one vantage point to get a clear view of the trout, and the area best suited to make a cast from is not the best for seeing the trout. So two anglers working together have an advantage. With good teamwork and great communication, your buddy can guide you where to cast and tell you when the trout has taken the fly.

The spotter and the caster need to have a system to communicate so that the caster can get into position, make the presentation, and set the hook using the spotter's eyes. Effective communication is essential; the wrong command by the spotter can mean lost fish for the caster.

The first step is to develop a system of voice commands. For example, some anglers refer to casting upstream as "cast higher," or "further upstream."

Two pairs of eyes are better than one. When you are hunting for trout, teamwork pays off. JACK HANRAHAN

When the trout eats, anglers use different terms like "set," "lift," and "it ate." Determine what voice commands the spotter will give so that you both know when to react. When anglers cannot see the trout, I have them point to the trout to get the correct location before they even make the cast.

Once the angler has pointed to the spot where the flies should land, make practice casts downstream of the trout. When the spotter has determined there is enough line out to make a cast, the caster should make a presentation to the area where the flies will eventually drift to the trout. If any adjustments are needed during the drift, or if the cast is off, the spotter can alert the caster to start over and make another cast.

For best results, both anglers should communicate throughout the process to ensure that they are on the same page. Teamwork reduces the chances that the trout will have the upper hand. Once you and your partner have developed good communication, the enjoyment of helping one another will shine through in every encounter with a trout. The buddy technique can be so effective that you will catch trout that you never would have considered without that extra set of eyes.

Teamwork Positioning

When using the buddy system, the caster does not have the best view of the trout—the spotter does. While this can take some getting used to, the casting angler does have the best possible approach on the river without having to spook the trout. Knowing how to approach the best position will increase the number of fish you can cast to.

Before you start, develop a plan. Most of the time, the spotter is in position on the high side of the river, or tucked into some cover in a camouflaged low position. The key for the spotter, once he or she is in place, is to not move. Don't point at the fish. Instead, verbally guide the casting angler's flies.

Once the spotter is in position and has a clear view of the trout, he guides the caster into the best position for making the cast, which should be close to the target. Next, the spotter lets the caster know what the best angle is to get the right presentation to the trout. A good way to communicate the correct angle is to use the clock system.

For example, if the angler is positioned below the trout and 12 o'clock is in front of his body, the spotter can explain how far to cast up- and across-stream, (for example, between 2 and 3 o'clock or at a 45-degree angle). These are the best commands to ensure the caster presents correctly to the trout. When the casting angler moves upstream to the correct position, the spotter needs to judge how low the caster needs to be when presenting the flies to the trout. Trust and communication are the keys.

Adjusting as a Team

Circumstances may require that the spotter and casting angler adjust the approach. When I am spotting a trout for a client and the cast is off, or if it lands so close to the trout it almost spooked, I will yell out, "Get it out of the water." Then I regroup with the casting angler to make sure the next drift is on point.

Adjust the cast if it is too long or too short. Having a view of the trout, the cast, the presentation, and the reaction of the fish allows the team to know what is happening. Every time I spot a fish for someone, I learn so much from seeing the

Double trouble: the trout did not stand a chance with this team on the water.

angler, the line, the trout, and the fight. When everything comes together, it is exciting.

Teamwork is also essential during the fight—most importantly at the end, when it is time to net the trout. Your partner can bridge the distance between you and the fish, allowing you the opportunity to net the trout in quickly. Having two extra hands is great when you are dealing with a large trout that is difficult to get close to.

The person fighting the fish needs to verbally guide the netting angler to let him know when the trout is ready for the net. If the trout is still applying power, netting the fish too early could result in a break off. Tell your partner it is still green, and wait for the fish to tire out more. The angler fighting the trout should remain upstream of the angler with the net to allow the trout to drift with the current to the net, preventing the fish from running in between his legs.

Use a net with a large opening and an extended handle. This is handy because the trout are usually not as tired when someone nets them for you. A long reach and big opening help you reach the trout and still keep a good distance from the fish to prevent the trout from wrapping the line around your legs when you take a stab at it.

Talk about what you are going to do as a team to get the fish in the net. This helps when you are fishing a run above a fast current or rapids that the trout will surely bolt toward. In these situations, we hook the fish and whoever has the net uses it to cover the opening to the fast water. We even go as far as slapping the long-handled net hard into the water, spooking the hooked trout to shoot upstream into water better for netting. Either way, these large nets are great for the buddy-system approach.

Teamwork can make or break many sight-fishing situations: having two pairs of eyes, two sets of hands—one with a rod, one with a net—is a huge advantage. In the end, the work of your team is what will get the fish into the net, especially handy when you are dealing with wary trout in tough conditions.

At the end of the fight it's time to net the trout. The angler fighting the trout must talk to the netting angler. When the trout starts to tire, let the netting angler go in and net the trout headfirst.

One of the most helpful tools to use with a partner is a good pair of walkie-talkies that have a range of a mile or two. This can be incredibly effective when covering a distance of water and while separated on the river. When someone spots a fish, call your partner on the walkie-talkie and then develop a game plan. During the spring and fall, I frequently use walkie-talkies to cover a large section of the water looking for migratory fish.

Consider getting a water-resistant model so you don't have to worry about moisture in bad weather conditions. The number of trout you see will double if you are covering water separately. Try it the next time you and your fishing partner are on the water.

Teamwork

The experience you share with your fishing partner is what really makes the trip. These memories will last a lifetime, told over and over again with the same passion and excitement as when you were on the water. You know that it was the teamwork that lead to spotting, hooking, fighting, and landing the trout. I know that I would not have had the satisfaction of enjoying the beauty of many trout without the help of my fishing friends.

The following story from Ross Purnell, editor of *Fly Fisherman*, illustrates the effectiveness of sight fishing.

"On a recent trip to Alberta's Bow River, my longtime friend Terry Johnson and I spent the better part of a morning taking turns perched high in the branches of an aspen tree. To the uninitiated, it seems like an unlikely place for a fly fisher. However, for those well versed in the buddy system it makes perfect sense.

"The tree was perched high on a steep outside corner of the riverbank and overlooked a shallow backwater. I began cautiously wading near the mouth of the backwater while Terry snuck through the bushes and clambered into the tree limbs.

"Although the water was shallow, the glare from the high sun prevented me from seeing the bottom even ten feet in front of me. Without eagle eyes up in the tree, I would not have bothered fishing this backwater. The water was flat and calm, and I knew the trout would be spooky.

"In a riffle you can prospect through the water until you find a fish—the turbulence of the water masks your footsteps as well as the splash of the line and fly. In this water, however, I needed the extra set of eyes not only to help me find the fish—but to avoid making casts and movements that might spook them.

"By now you can probably guess what happened. Terry spotted a cruising 20-inch Bow River rainbow. He directed my cast away from the trout to avoid spooking it, and the fly landed about 30 feet away from the approaching trout, but right along the weed bed the fish seemed to be following.

"Terry called the event like a radio announcer: 'The fish just picked something up near the bottom. Now he is moving forward. He is 20 feet away. He is moving out toward the main river now . . . no, he's moving back along the weed bed. He is 10 feet away from your hopper and coming straight at you. He sees the fly, HE'S SPEEDING UP!' Slurp.

"Fishing with a friend or a guide in this fashion is one of the most rewarding, fascinating ways to catch fish. I will not make a blanket statement and say you will catch more fish (one person is always NOT fishing); however, you can learn more fishing this way than you ever will fishing blind. When I fish this way with my friends, the spotter is often the prized position. Sure, the person with the rod gets to reel the fish in (the manual labor), but the spotter gets all the visual entertainment and directs the fishing like an orchestra.

"To make this kind of buddy fishing work, you need good water clarity and a high vantage point. A tree works great because you can look out through the leaves and branches, but the trout cannot see you. All the trout sees is the same tree that has always been there.

"However, trees are not always climbable or in the right spot. Many high outside banks in the West have nothing more than prairie grass, so approach them carefully. Poke your head up high enough only to obtain a line of sight to where the trout is. There's no need to silhouette your whole body against the horizon. Avoid throwing any kind of a shadow on the water, and whenever possible, use rocks, trees, and shrubs to mask your movements and outline.

"In the East, trees are more likely to be a problem than your savior, as there are often so many you cannot get a good look into the stream bottom.

"In stillwater situations (as described above) the trout will be moving. You will cast very little to avoid spooking the trout, and your buddy will direct you to cast well in front of the advancing fish.

"In rivers and streams, the trout sit in one position and wait for food to come to them. In many instances, the water is slightly roiled and there is little danger of spooking the trout. The big chal-

From spotting to landing to photographing this fish, teamwork was key. JAY NICHOLS

It took teamwork and communication from all of us on the water to land this quality trout. We figured out that the trout were keying in on streamers. Ross Purnell displays one of the many great trout we enjoyed that day on the water. ROSS PURNELL

lenge is not stealth but in getting the fly to the bottom and directly into the fish's feeding lane.

"Your spotter should be above and down-stream of the trout (to avoid spooking the fish), and you should be in the water behind the fish. If you can, stand to one side of the fish or the other so that your line never passes directly over the head of the fish.

"The fish may be three feet deep or more, so you will have to cast well upstream of the fish (ten feet or more) to allow your weighted flies to sink to the level of the trout. Add too much split shot and the weight will make the flies move unnaturally slow, or sometimes the split shot itself can spook the fish.

"Your buddy watching the fish will be more helpful if he can see your fly, so try adding an in-dicator nymph like an egg pattern or small piece of indicator yarn just 12 to 18 inches away from your fly. This way he can more accurately judge whether your fly is getting close to the fish or not, and he can give you better casting instructions. In cases like this he will not be directing your casts right at the fish but at a target area upstream of the fish that will presumably drift the fly down the correct feeding lane and allow time for the fly to sink.

"With this many variables, you will often need many casts and a great deal of feedback from your buddy. In addition to watching the fly (if possible), your buddy should watch the fish closely. When the fly passes close to the fish, watch for sudden movement to the left or right, or the white flash of the mouth opening and closing. If you are fishing blind, the fish can (and will) eat and then spit out your fly without you ever recognizing a strike. With a buddy, you can eliminate these types of misses by watching the fish closely and yelling 'strike' when you see the fish make a predatory movement."

The best parts of any fly-fishing adventure are the experiences you share with friends and fellow anglers along the way. This is especially true when you are working as a team, sight fishing for trout. The satisfaction of knowing that the trout was caught by the combined efforts of you and your fishing partner is invigorating, giving each of you a sense of accomplishment—no matter who landed the trout.

Collaboration with friends on and off the water will help you grow as a sight angler. I am constantly challenging myself, and I find that I learn something new each day I am on the water. There is so much to see and experience while sight fishing. If you take the time to hunt for trout, you *will* catch more fish. You will also focus more on the trout, and less on the distractions (like strike indicators on your rig).

Always look before you fish. You will be a better angler—and the excitement of seeing the takes will keep you coming back for more.

Index